OLDEST CINCINNATI

Rick Pender (signature)

RICK PENDER

REEDY PRESS

Library of Congress Control Number: 2020950062

ISBN: 9781681063041

Cover Design: Jill Halpin
Book Design: Linda Eckels

Cover photo credits, clockwise from top left: Roebling Suspension Bridge (Chuck Eilerman/Story Project); Memorial Hall (Barberstock/Cincinnati Region); Cincinnati City Hall (Public Domain); Music Hall (Cincinnati Symphony Orchestra).

Printed in the United States of America
21 22 23 24 25   5 4 3 2 1

Dedication

To my parents Frank and Merle Pender. He was a renaissance handyman, able and willing to do many things, not unlike the pioneers who built Cincinnati. She had a curiosity about the world that lit a fire in me to always be reading and learning more. Their model of hard work and generous spirits, as well as my happy boyhood home, were the perfect foundation for my own pursuits.

TABLE OF CONTENTS

OVER-THE-RHINE

Mount Adams and Eden Park

North

EAST

WEST

ACKNOWLEDGMENTS

Throughout my years of synthesizing and writing about Cincinnati history and giving tours to visitors, I've drawn upon many sources. Don Heinrich Tolzmann and Mike Morgan's books about beer and German brewers were essential, as were two volumes, *The Bicentennial Guide to Greater Cincinnati*, published in 1988 by the Cincinnati Historical Society. I must single out two individuals in particular. One is historian extraordinaire Dan Hurley, who gave me insightful guidance early on and pointed me toward items that were new to me. Dan also warned against jumping to conclusions about what's old — when something older might materialize in the process of digging deeper. The other is *Cincinnati Enquirer* archivist and local historian Jeff Suess. His books, especially *Cincinnati: An Illustrated Timeline* and *Cincinnati: Then and Now*, were constant resources. In addition, Jeff gave me access to many of the wonderful photos used to illustrate *Oldest Cincinnati*. I'm especially grateful for both of these generous men.

INTRODUCTION

Cincinnati is an old city, at least by American standards. It is, in fact, the oldest city in what was the Northwest Territory, established in 1787. From that land, four states were eventually carved: Ohio (1803), Indiana (1816), Illinois (1818), Michigan (1837), and Wisconsin (1848). Fort Washington, the first military outpost in the territory, was established in 1789. Via the Ohio River, restless residents of the original 13 colonies and ambitious immigrants from the British Isles began heading west in the late 18th century to Cincinnati, founded in 1788. By the early 19th century Cincinnati, the first city founded after the American Revolution, was booming. As the first major inland city in the US, it was one of the most populated in the US as of 1840.

That was when German immigrants flocked to the city that resembled Munich. The Ohio River Valley was reminiscent of the Rhine Valley in Bavaria, and the climate was similar. In 1840 the city's population included just 3,500 German-born people, seven percent of the total population. By 1850, 23,000 people of German descent were 20 percent of the city's population. In 1870, 73,000 Germans accounted for 35 percent. By 1890 Cincinnati's population of 300,000 included 174,000 people who were German-born or of German descent, fully 58 percent of the people living here. They left an indelible cultural impression on the Queen City of the West, one that still resonates in the 21st century.

Beyond the impact of German immigration, several individuals shaped Cincinnati's history well beyond singular events or institutions: physician Daniel Drake, landowner Nicholas Longworth and his arts-and-culture granddaughter Maria Longworth Nichols Storer, and architect Samuel Hannaford. Keep an eye out for them in notes attached to many of the entries. You'll also notice some particularly important people and places integral to Cincinnati's history are highlighted in bold.

Cincinnati is a fascinating American city, and this book recounts 90 of its oldest things that represent a rich tapestry of accomplishment, achievement, and pride. It's been a genuine delight to assemble *Oldest Cincinnati*. I invite you to share in the pleasure.

KENTUCKY

OLDEST RELICS
BIG BONE LICK STATE PARK
3380 Beaver Rd., Union, KY

I n Union, Kentucky, 25 miles south of Cincinnati, there is evidence of creatures that walked the earth more than 16,000 years ago: In the 1770s, Nicholas Cresswell (1750–1804) found fossilized bones of "prodigious size," especially tusk fragments and teeth (one weighing 10 pounds), leading him to call the place the "Big Elephant Lick." President Thomas Jefferson sent William Clark (1770–1838) to collect bones there in 1807, shortly after he and Meriwether Lewis (1774–1809) conducted their legendary expedition across the American West. Over the years, Big Bone Lick State Park, established in 1960 and listed in 1972 on the National Register of Historic Places as well as in 2009 as a National Natural Landmark, came to be thought of as the site where American paleontology began.

The bones Cresswell unearthed were Ice Age remains of woolly mammoths, as well as mastodons, bison, caribou, deer, moose, musk oxen, and others. They were drawn by a salt lick created by sulfur springs. The swampy surrounding land trapped these large animals, with no way to escape.

The park's visitor center has exhibits of fossils, both indoors and

outside, including a half-ton mastodon skull. There are several trails for exploring the 525-acre park, especially a boardwalk with a "Megafauna diorama" with interpretive panels around a marsh bog, illustrating how animals used the site and became victims. The park maintains an American bison herd, viewable year-round. There also are picnic areas, an 18-hole miniature golf course, playgrounds, tennis courts, and a 62-site campground with a swimming pool.

Big Bone Lick Park is an official Lewis and Clark Heritage Trail Site. It features several easily accessed nature trails across diverse habitats, including grassland, wetland, and savanna.

Photo courtesy of Kentucky State Parks.

10,000 BC

OLDEST ROADS
DIXIE HIGHWAY
US 127/US 42/US 25

There's been a lot of discussion of the "Dixie Highway" in Northern Kentucky, known as US 127/US 42/US 25, as well as KY 17. Its history goes back a century to Carl Fisher (1874–1939), an entrepreneur who promoted a route for travel from northern states to Miami Beach between 1915 and 1927. The "Dixie" nomenclature became controversial in light of concerns surrounding racism in 2020.

But Kentucky roads have a much more distant history: This highway's path was first blazed by American bison—often called buffalo—migrating north and south around 10,000 BC. Herds of these large mammals grazed the plains in what's now mid-Ohio during the summer. In the fall they migrated south, crossing the Ohio River at its lowest ebb at a natural limestone ford at the mouth of Kentucky's Licking River. They probably were attracted by salt licks caused by saline springs along the banks of the Licking and elsewhere in Kentucky.

Over time, these migrations compacted the soil into trails. Indigenous people lived across the river's watershed and hunted these large beasts for food, clothing, and shelter. Several "Great Buffalo Roads" converged where the Licking joined the larger Ohio River. Wild bison eventually were hunted to near extinction around 1800 AD. A contemporary herd of bison is maintained at **Big Bone Lick State Park** in Union, Kentucky.

One might even say that Northern Kentucky's first traffic engineers were bison. The history of these routes is portrayed in the first of Robert Dafford's 18 Roebling Murals on the floodwall at the Covington riverfront, adjacent to the **Roebling Suspension Bridge**.

The Roebling Murals, created by artist Robert Dafford, were painted between 2002 and 2005 on the Covington floodwall, just west of the historic Roebling Suspension Bridge.

Photo courtesy of Rick Pender.

OLDEST FERRY
AUGUSTA FERRY AUTHORITY
201 Seminary Ave., Augusta, KY
augustaky.com/augusta-ferry

ANDERSON FERRY
4030 River Rd., Hebron, KY
One Anderson Ferry Rd., Cincinnati
andersonferryofficial.com

The Augusta Ferry, the region's oldest continuously operating ferry service between Ohio and Kentucky, is based in the charming town of Augusta, Kentucky, 45 miles east on the Ohio River. John Boude began shuttling passengers between Kentucky and Ohio using his hand-propelled ferry on April 2, 1798, just a few months after the town was chartered by the Kentucky legislature in October 1797. In the 21st

Photo courtesy of nkyviews.com.

century the diesel-powered Jenny Ann transports people and vehicles from the south shore (KY State Route 8) to a landing one mile west of Higginsport, Ohio (US 52). It's the only public river crossing for a 55-mile stretch between Cincinnati and Maysville, Kentucky. Passage for a car is $5; riders on foot go free if a paying vehicle is on board.

Photo courtesy of ohio981.blogspot.com.

Plying the Ohio closer to Cincinnati is another historic service, the Anderson Ferry, which began operating on March 3, 1817, transporting riders from Constance, Kentucky, to the Ohio River's north bank, about seven miles west of downtown Cincinnati. It was nearly a half-century before the **Roebling Suspension Bridge** opened. The ferry was registered on the National Register of Historic Places in 1982. Nine different boats, all named "Boone," in honor of Boone County, Kentucky, have served travelers for more than two centuries. The wooden Boone No. 1 was literally horse-powered, with animals walking on a treadmill. Still in service is Boone No. 7, launched in 1937, the first-ever, steam-powered ferry made of steel; its power was upgraded with the first diesel marine engine a decade later. About 300 cars are transported daily. Boone No. 9 joined the fleet in 1993. Cars travel for $5, foot passengers are 50 cents, bicycles are $1, motorcycles are $2, cash only.

The Freedom Center is situated directly north of the Roebling Suspension Bridge, just steps from the Ohio River. That natural barrier separated the slave states of the South from the free states of the North.

OLDEST REMNANT OF SLAVERY
NATIONAL UNDERGROUND RAILROAD FREEDOM CENTER
50 E Freedom Way

The National Underground Railroad Freedom Center in downtown Cincinnati has a sobering historical exhibit: a 21-by-30-foot slave pen recovered from a farm in Mason County, Kentucky, less than 60 miles away. It's the oldest remnant of slavery that can be seen locally. Built around 1830, the structure was used as a holding pen by Capt. John W. Anderson, a slave trader. He bought his farmstead in 1825 and was active in the slave trade in the 1830s. He held enslaved people in the pen until he had at least 30 to take to market in Mississippi or Louisiana. Most people auctioned there were forced into back-breaking work at cotton plantations. Male slaves were kept on the pen's upper floor, inhumanely shackled to rings that prevented escape. Women and children were held on the pen's lower floor. Its few windows were covered in iron bars but left open to the elements. Anderson died in 1835 while chasing a runaway slave. He had made a small fortune, which financed his horse breeding business.

The Freedom Center, which opened in 2004, is worth an extended visit to experience stories about freedom's heroes and to understand better the painful realities of slavery and injustice from the era of the Underground Railroad to contemporary times. It's a "museum of conscience," similar to the United States Holocaust Memorial Museum in Washington, DC.

Photo courtesy of National Underground Railroad Freedom Center.

OLDEST BRIDGE
JOHN A. ROEBLING SUSPENSION BRIDGE
Connecting Downtown Covington to Downtown Cincinnati
roeblingbridge.org

Johann August Röbling was born in Mühlhausen, Prussia, and immigrated at age 25 to the United States, where he Americanized his name to John A. Roebling (1806–1869) and became a civil engineer. He's most remembered as the designer of the Brooklyn Bridge (1883), but he got his start with a smaller but similarly impressive structure, the Cincinnati-Covington Bridge. The prototype for its famous descendant, its name today honors its engineer. The John A. Roebling Suspension Bridge was the first permanent bridge across the Ohio River. When it was completed in 1866, it was the longest suspension bridge in the world. It is Cincinnati's oldest bridge.

Construction began in 1856 but stalled after an 1857 bank panic. A series of bridge failures elsewhere in the region shook public confidence. Wrangling between political leaders in Ohio and Kentucky about aligning downtown streets between Cincinnati and Covington created more delays. By the time the Civil War started, the bridge's foundations were completed, but the argument postponed further work. The necessity to move Union troops across the river got things going again, and the 230-feet-tall bridge towers were completed in 1865, defining a span of 1,030 feet. It took months to string the cables, some more than a foot in diameter. On December 2, 1866, the

Photo courtesy of Story Project.

day after the bridge opened, 120,000 people walked across the Ohio River.

During the 1937 flood, the bridge was the only one to remain open across the Ohio between Cairo, Illinois, and Steubenville, Ohio, a distance of approximately 600 miles. Originally built with horse-drawn vehicles in mind, today it's limited to cars—no buses or trucks. Despite occasional closures and repairs, the Roebling Suspension Bridge is a lasting, iconic symbol of the connections between Kentucky and Ohio. It became a National Historic Landmark in 1975.

The Suspension Bridge is an engineering marvel. Its two primary cables each contain 5,180 individual wires that were "spun" in place. The wire was imported from England.

OLDEST COUNTY COURTHOUSE
CAMPBELL COUNTY COURTHOUSE

330 York St., Newport, KY
campbellcountyky.gov

The Campbell County Courthouse in Newport, Kentucky, dates from 1884, when it was referred to as "a temple of justice." Built on the site of the county's first two courthouses, a wood-frame structure from 1797 and a two-story brick building from 1815, the 1884 building is one of the largest and most architecturally distinctive courthouses in the Commonwealth of Kentucky. Designed by Cincinnati architect A.C. Nash (1826–1890) and Newport, Kentucky architect L.H. Wilson (1857–1935), the courthouse's High Victorian architecture features a tall, four-sided clock-and-bell tower, stylized masonry details, a marble interior staircase, and an ornate, allegorical, cathedral-style stained glass window. The building sits on a natural rise at the junction of two major streets and faces a tree-shaded green. It was named to the National Register of Historic Places in 1980.

Campbell County is unusual in that it has two county seats. In 1840 Kentucky's General Assembly designated Alexandria, 12 miles south of Newport, as the official county seat, and a red-brick courthouse was built there. It holds many historic records still, including papers signed by Daniel Boone and Henry Clay.

In 1883, after lengthy lobbying, the General Assembly allowed Newport to designate a courthouse district beyond Alexandria. It was not until 2010 that Newport was granted equal status.

Several other historic buildings are near the courthouse: St. Paul's Episcopal Church at York Street and Court Place (1874, National Register, 1980); Thompson-Southgate House at 24 E Third St. (1814, National Register, 1976); and the Salem United Methodist Church at 802 York St. (1882, National Register, 1986), known since 1988 as the Stained Glass Theatre and operated by a community theater group, Footlighters, Inc.

Just steps from the courthouse is the World Peace Bell, one of the world's largest free-swinging bells. It weighs 66,000 pounds, including a three-ton clapper. It's rung daily at noon.

Photo courtesy of Rick Pender.

OLDEST AMPHITHEATERS

DEVOU PARK
1201 Park Dr., Covington, KY

SEASONGOOD PAVILION
1600 Art Museum Dr., Eden Park

Greater Cincinnati has several amphitheaters designed for outdoor entertainment. The oldest is in Devou Park in Covington, Kentucky, opened in 1939, a Works Progress Administration (WPA) construction project. The 700-acre park with a panoramic view of the Cincinnati skyline and the Ohio River once was a family farm owned by William and Sarah Devou. In 1910, their children donated the estate to the city of Covington.

The band shell, nestled on a grassy bowl in the park's rolling hills, is a versatile venue for weddings, receptions, awards ceremonies, and more. In its inaugural summer, the band shell drew a crowd of 40,000, the largest ever recorded in the park. Today it is the home of the Kentucky Symphony Orchestra's popular summer series, where concertgoers spread out on the grassy hillside to picnic and enjoy the music.

In Ohio, Eden Park's Seasongood Pavilion was established as a venue in 1960 on a site where three previous bandstands had hosted entertainment since 1872. Situated in a tree-shaded bowl across from the Cincinnati Art Museum and below the Playhouse in the Park, the natural amphitheater was named for

Photo courtesy of exploredovoupark.org.

Murray Seasongood (1878–1983). He authored the Cincinnati City Charter (1925) and served as Cincinnati's mayor from 1926 to 1930. For many years he was president of the national Legal Aid Society. The concrete pavilion, a gift to the city from Seasongood's sister, Martha S. Stern, is a popular spot for free summertime concerts and occasional theatrical presentations, including plays by Shakespeare. Attendees can sit on rows of park benches or on the hillside.

Also found in Devou Park is the Behringer-Crawford Museum, a regional center for the collection, presentation, study, and enjoyment of the Ohio Valley's natural, cultural, visual, and performing arts heritage.

DOWNTOWN

Oldest Park
Piatt Park
100 Garfield Pl.

In April 1817, John H. Piatt (1781–1822), an early Cincinnati entrepreneur involved in steamboat construction, insurance, banking, and real estate speculation, and his brother, Benjamin M. Piatt (1779–1863), a lawyer and judge in the Hamilton County Common Pleas Court, donated two blocks of downtown property to the city for a marketplace. Due to its proximity to other markets, the land instead became Cincinnati's first city park. It had no name until 1868, when it was dedicated as Eighth Street Park.

That lasted until 1882, when it was named Garfield Park in memory of President James A. Garfield, an Ohio native, who was assassinated in 1881. Garfield's statue by Charles H. Niehaus (1855–1935) was unveiled in 1887 and placed at the intersection of Race and Eighth Streets. An equestrian statue by Louis T. Rebisso (1837–1899) of another president with

Photo courtesy of Rick Pender.

Ohio ties, William Henry Harrison, was placed at the park's opposite end in 1895. Harrison and John Piatt were good friends early in the century. With the advent of automobiles, Garfield's statue in the middle of a busy street became a traffic hazard, so it was moved in 1904 to the west end of the park at Elm Street. In October 1940, the park was renamed to honor the Piatts. In 1988, a renovation resulted in the statues trading places.

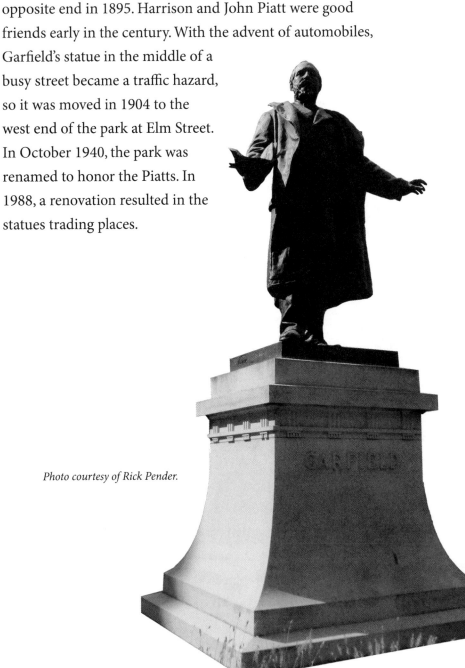

Photo courtesy of Rick Pender.

OLDEST STORE
BROMWELL'S
117 W 4th St.
bromwells.com

Bromwell's, a fireplace and home décor shop, is the oldest store in downtown Cincinnati, in business for more than 200 years. Jacob Bromwell (1785–1866) came to Cincinnati on a flatboat in 1819 and established a company manufacturing wire goods and housewares. His catalog listed more than 1,000 products, and his store occupied six floors of a building at 181 Walnut St., just a few steps north of the Ohio River. His

Photo courtesy of Rick Pender.

company patented the world's first flour sifter, and one of its best-selling items was a popcorn popper. Bromwell created many other metal products, including tin cups for soldiers in both armies during the Civil War.

In 1923 the company split into a housewares division that moved to Indiana and a fireplace division that remained in Cincinnati. Today, the fireplace store is located on West Fourth Street in the city's downtown. Jeff McClorey, Bromwell's owner since 2005, has sustained the company's reputation for fine décor, focusing on fireplaces and related home furnishings.

—1820
OLDEST DOWNTOWN HOME
TAFT MUSEUM OF ART
316 Pike St.
taftmuseum.org

The Taft Museum of Art occupies the oldest home in downtown, built by Martin Baum (1765–1831), a manufacturer and banker. As Cincinnati's first millionaire, he spearheaded the founding of an early public library, a literary society, and the Western Museum with **Dr. Daniel Drake**. He wanted a home to match his reputation and undertook work on Belmont Square, a handsome, Federal-style, wood-frame structure, completed by 1820. However, Baum's wealth evaporated during a financial panic in 1819, and it's probable he never lived there. A bank took over the property and leased it to a "school for young ladies" for several years.

In 1829, Belmont was purchased by another Cincinnati millionaire, banker and winemaker **Nicholas Longworth**. In 1851, he hired Robert S. Duncanson, America's first well-known African American painter, to create large landscapes on the plaster walls of the entryway. His murals, covered with wallpaper in the 1860s, were restored when the Taft Museum opened in 1931.

David Sinton (1808–1900) became the owner in 1869. An Irish immigrant who came to America at age 3, he made a fortune selling iron, then invested in a successful downtown hotel. When he died in 1900, his daughter, Anna (1850–1931), and her husband, Charles P. Taft (1843–1929), became the owners. Charles was the editor of the *Cincinnati Times-Star* and owner of two professional baseball teams. His younger half-brother, **William Howard Taft** (1857–1930), was America's 27th president (1909–1913) and the tenth chief justice of the US Supreme Court (1921–1930); he delivered his 1908 presidential nomination acceptance speech from the building's portico. Charles and Anna amassed a spectacular art collection, including works by Corot, Rembrandt, Gainsborough, and Cincinnati painter Frank Duveneck. In 1927, they bequeathed the building and its art collection to the city as the Taft Museum.

Photo courtesy of Rick Pender.

OLDEST LIBRARY

MERCANTILE LIBRARY
414 Walnut St.
mercantilelibrary.com

CINCINNATI & HAMILTON COUNTY PUBLIC LIBRARY
800 Vine St.
cincinnatilibrary.org

LLOYD LIBRARY AND MUSEUM
917 Plum St.
lloydLibrary.org

A s Cincinnati became a cultured city, libraries were important. In April 1835, young professional men gathered to establish the Young Men's Mercantile Library, requiring paid memberships. It was located in the Cincinnati College building on Walnut Street. Today it's on the 11th and 12th stories of the Mercantile Library Building on Walnut Street, constructed in 1908 on the site of the onetime college. After a serious 1845 fire, the library made its $10,000 rent payment to help the college

Photo courtesy of Caroline R. Gautier from Mercantile Library,

rebuild. Its appreciative leaders granted the library a 10,000-year, renewable lease.

The Mercantile's 80,000-volume collection includes contemporary fiction, nonfiction, classics, history, poetry, and

Photo courtesy of Rick Pender.

travel. It has presented dynamic lecturers, writers, and speakers on topics such as politics, art, literature, science, and religion. In particular, the "Merc" has a long history of hosting renowned authors, including Herman Melville, Ralph Waldo Emerson, Harriet Beecher Stowe, John Updike, Julia Child, and Toni Morrison. Its reading room with glass-floored stacks and tall, arched windows is a downtown oasis for readers, intellectuals, and informed citizens.

North of the Mercantile is the Cincinnati Public Library, established in 1853 after beginning in 1802 as a subscription library. Old Main (1874), its magnificent original building, stood at the intersection of Vine and Seventh streets. It lasted until 1955, when a new, contemporary facility opened at 800 Vine St. Expanded twice, it is the central branch of 41 locations constituting the Public Library of Cincinnati and Hamilton County.

Lloyd Library began as the personal collection of books belonging to pharmacist John Uri Lloyd (1849–1936). It contains resources about medical botany, pharmacy, eclectic medicine, and horticulture. Lloyd and his brothers established trusts to support the library. The current location (1970) is open to the public and free of charge.

OLDEST MANUFACTURER
THE PROCTER & GAMBLE COMPANY
1 P&G Plaza
pg.com

William Cooper Procter (1801–1884), a "candle molder," and James Norris Gamble (1803–1891), a "soap boiler," married a pair of sisters, Olivia and Elizabeth Norris, in 1837. Their father encouraged his sons-in-law to become business partners that year. Their businesses were rooted in tallow, a fatty byproduct of Cincinnati's thriving pork industry.

Within 20 years, Procter & Gamble had 80 employees and sales of $1 million. During the Civil War, it supplied the Union Army with soap and candles. The first company offices were at Sixth and Main streets, not far from P&G's current world headquarters. In 1879, Gamble's son, a chemist, developed an inexpensive floating soap called Ivory, for which advertising began nationally in 1882. After the manufacturing plant

Photos courtesy of P&G Heritage & Archives Center.

on Central Avenue burned in 1884, it was replaced by a new factory, Ivorydale, with buildings that still stand in St. Bernard. A memorial sculpture (1934) of William Cooper Procter stands in front of the Ivorydale Technical Center.

Photo courtesy of P&G Heritage & Archives Center.

With more than 10,000 local employees, P&G in the 21st century is a global company, producing and expertly marketing an extensive array of consumer products sold nationally and internationally. More than 20 of its 50-plus brands—including Tide laundry detergent, Crest toothpaste, Dawn dishwashing liquid, Febreze odor eliminator, Gillette razors, Bounty paper towels, Pampers disposable diapers, and Charmin bathroom tissue—have annual sales in excess of $1 billion. A prolific developer of products, the company has sold more than 50 renowned brands to other companies, including Crisco vegetable oil, Folgers coffee, Jif peanut butter, Noxzema skin cream, Oxydol laundry detergent, Pringles potato chips, and Spic and Span floor cleaner.

Procter & Gamble's downtown Cincinnati corporate headquarters spans two blocks along East 5th Street. The buildings are fronted by beautifully maintained green space framed by pergolas topped with wisteria.

Oldest Cathedrals
St. Peter in Chains Cathedral
325 W 8th St.
stpeterinchainscathedral.org

St. Mary's Cathedral Basilica of the Assumption
1140 Madison Ave., Covington, KY
covcathedral.com

The cornerstone for St. Peter in Chains, downtown's dignified Roman Catholic cathedral, was laid in 1841. It was the second permanent cathedral in the United States and is acknowledged as the nation's oldest cathedral built as a cathedral that remains in use. Classic Corinthian columns line the stately

Photo courtesy of Rick Pender.

portico; it has a towering, 225-foot, octagonal steeple with a clock and bells. The church lost its cathedral status in 1938, due to a decreasing number of parishioners. It was reinstated as the archdiocesan cathedral in 1951, just ahead of an expansion and $5 million renovation. The interior features Greek-styled mosaics with Venetian glass and distinctive murals of the stations of the cross. The cathedral's name derives from a work by Spanish painter Bartolomé Esteban Murillo (1617–1682) of an angel liberating St. Peter from prison. In 2020, Pope Francis designated the cathedral as a minor basilica.

Another beautiful place of worship is Covington's Cathedral Basilica of the Assumption, which opened to worshipers in 1901 and serves as the cathedral of the Northern Kentucky diocese. Its west limestone façade is a replica, complete with gargoyles, of Notre Dame Cathedral in Paris. The interior, modeled on the Basilica of Saint-Denis, a medieval cathedral in suburban Paris, features 82 stained glass windows, including one of the world's largest (24 by 67 feet), a depiction of the Council of Ephesus in 431 AD that proclaimed Mary as the Mother of God. Fourteen painstakingly detailed ceramic mosaic panels depict the stations of the cross; the sanctuary also features murals painted by renowned artist Frank Duveneck (1848–1919), a Covington native.

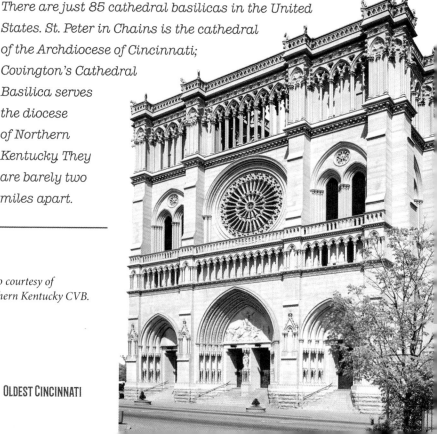

There are just 85 cathedral basilicas in the United States. St. Peter in Chains is the cathedral of the Archdiocese of Cincinnati; Covington's Cathedral Basilica serves the diocese of Northern Kentucky. They are barely two miles apart.

Photo courtesy of Northern Kentucky CVB.

Oldest Literary Club
The Literary Club

550 E 4th St.
cincylit.org

The oldest literary club in the United States meets regularly in an 1820 building adjacent to Lytle Park in downtown's southeast corner. Founded on October 29, 1849, The Literary Club has operated since 1850 with a membership of men who share papers they have written on literary or historic topics.

Prior to its present location, the club met at various downtown locations. In 1929, club member Charles Phelps Taft, who lived in the building that's today's **Taft Museum of Art**, purchased the two-story, 19th-century, Greek Revival–style building, a private home for more than a century. The club remodeled the building and signed a 99-year lease for $1 per year on June 27, 1930. The first club meeting there was June 30, 1930. The Literary Club purchased the house outright on July 17, 1951.

Photo courtesy of Rick Pender.

Past members included US Presidents Rutherford B. Hayes and **William Howard Taft**, philanthropist **Nicholas Longworth**, who lived in the Taft Museum building prior to Charles and Anna Taft, artist Frank Duveneck, and several presidents of the University of Cincinnati. Past guests included essayist Ralph Waldo Emerson, civil rights advocate Booker T. Washington, novelist Mark Twain, playwright Oscar Wilde, and several poets, including Matthew Arnold, Robert Frost, Randall Jarrell, and Stephen Spender.

The brass plate affixed to the club's front door was created in 1889. When the 4th Street building was acquired in 1929, "The Literary Club" plaque was re-installed there.

Oldest Professional Fire Department

Cincinnati Fire Museum

315 W Court St.
cincyfiremuseum.com

In 1803, the same year Ohio became a state, Cincinnati established a night watch of volunteers to fight fires. Numerous independent fire companies vied for business during the first decades of the 19th century. In 1853, after 10 different companies arrived at a lumberyard fire and fought a brawl instead of the blaze, a paid, professional fire department was established. Other cities had firefighters, but Cincinnati had a department made up of full-time employees. It was the first in the United States to employ a steam engine in firefighting. Cincinnati's contemporary department has a long tradition of excellence in its training programs.

The history of local firefighting is chronicled at the Cincinnati Fire Museum in the former Engine House No. 45 (1906) in downtown Cincinnati. A fine example of Renaissance Revival architecture, it was a busy station until the mid-20th century. Often, it was the first responder to fires in downtown and in the West End, where homes, tenements, commercial, and industrial buildings were closely packed. It closed in 1962 and opened as a museum in December 1980.

Photo courtesy of Rick Pender.

OLDEST BANK
FIFTH THIRD BANK
38 Fountain Sq. Plaza

The Fifth Third Bank's name often leads to curious questions. But its long history makes it Cincinnati's oldest bank. In 1858, William W. Scarborough founded the Bank of the Ohio Valley in the city's financial district on Third Street. Its noble purpose was to improve the lives of customers and communities through sound banking principles and superior service. Thirteen years later, in 1871, it was acquired by the Third National Bank. Another institution, the Queen City National Bank, changed its name to the Fifth National Bank in 1888. It merged with Third National in 1909, creating the Fifth-Third Bank, with a hyphen that eventually was dropped. Prohibition began not long after the merger, and legend has it that "Fifth Third" was preferable to "Third Fifth," which could have been construed as a reference to three-fifths of liquor.

In 1977, Fifth Third introduced Jeanie, the first online shared network of ATMs in the United States. The bank's tall, vertical façade was featured in the opening credits of the TV sitcom *WKRP in Cincinnati* (1978–1982) as the backdrop for the Tyler Davidson Fountain on Fountain Square.

In 2019, the Fifth Third History Museum, a corporate museum, opened at the bank's headquarters in downtown Cincinnati on Walnut Street. Fifth Third is the city's largest locally based bank and the ninth-largest US-based consumer bank.

Photo courtesy of Rick Pender.

OLDEST SYNAGOGUES
SHERITH ISRAEL SYNAGOGUE
625 Ruth Lyons Ln.

ISAAC M. WISE TEMPLE
720 Plum St.
wisetemple.org

The first synagogue in Cincinnati was Sherith Israel Temple. The 1861 building remains on a downtown back street, although it ceased to be a place of worship in 1882. It subsequently served as a warehouse, plumbing supply house, and a machine shop. Today, it contains several condominiums. Nevertheless, it's remembered as the oldest existing Orthodox Jewish synagogue west of the Allegheny Mountains. It's also the fourth-oldest building in downtown Cincinnati and the seventh-oldest synagogue structure in the United States.

In 1866, not long after Sherith Israel Temple was built, a much grander synagogue was established: the Isaac M. Wise Temple, now often called the Plum Street Temple. Cincinnati became a center of national Jewish life around the time of the Civil War, and Rabbi Isaac Mayer Wise (1819–1900) was its leader. He founded American Reformed Judaism, the most liberal form of the Jewish faith, and was the founder and first president of **Hebrew Union College** (1875). In the 1860s, the families of the temple K.K. B'nai Yeshurun purchased land at Eighth and Plum streets and hired architect James Keys Wilson to design their new temple. It was built at a cost of $263,525.

Keys used a Byzantine-Moorish architectural style that was used for several German synagogues in the 19th century, recalling the Jewish faith's golden age in Spain. The temple's design reflected Rabbi Wise's optimism that the American Jewish experience would become another golden age. Especially noteworthy are twin minarets reminiscent of Islamic architecture, a

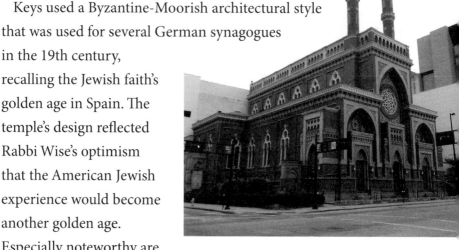

Isaac M. Wise Temple.
Photo courtesy of Rick Pender.

beautiful rose window, and the temple's original pipe organ. With seating for 1,400, the ornately stenciled sanctuary features 14 bands of Hebrew text, primarily from the Book of Psalms.

The temple was placed on the National Register of Historic Places in 1975. From 1994 to 1995, it underwent extensive restoration.

Sherith Israel Synagogue.
Photo courtesy of Rick Pender.

Oldest Bar
Arnold's Bar and Grill
210 E 8th St.
arnoldsbarandgrill.com

O'Malley's in the Alley
25 Ogden Pl.
omalleyscincy.com

In 1861, Simon Arnold opened Arnold's Bar in a pair of side-by-side, red brick buildings. Built in the late 1830s, they operated as a whorehouse, then a barbershop, and finally a feed store. The courtyard first was used as a stable and a carriage house. When Hugo Arnold operated the bar in the early 20th century, he and his family lived on the second floor, now dining rooms. During Prohibition, a kitchen was added, establishing Arnold's as both a grill and a bar. An old bathtub, purportedly used to make gin, remains on the second floor. The popularity of the city's oldest continuously operating bar was ramped up by colorful owner Jim Tarbell in 1976; he turned the courtyard into an outdoor patio, roofed over and heated for year-round use, with a porch-like stage for live music.

The bar's historic interior décor is an eye-popping welter of old-school fixtures, dark wood, historic photos, and posters. The courtyard is a popular hangout for politicians awaiting results on election night. Every March, Cincinnati's annual Bockfest Parade kicks off at Arnold's before proceeding up Main Street for Over-the-Rhine's celebration of bock beer.

Another historic downtown drinkery is O'Malley's in the Alley, sometimes called downtown's "Oldest Hole-in-the-Wall" destination. Since 1892 it's been wedged into a block between Race and Vine streets just south of Fourth Street, sometimes going by other names including Ogden's Place and The Hideaway. It's been referred to humorously as that out-of-the-way place where nobody goes, but usually has a crowd.

Photo courtesy of Rick Pender.

Oldest Professional Baseball Team

Great American Ball Park

100 Joe Nuxhall Way
mlb.com/reds/ballpark

Cincinnati Reds Hall of Fame and Museum

443 E Pete Rose Way, Great American Ball Park
mlb.com/reds/hall-of-fame

The Cincinnati Red Stockings began playing baseball in 1869, the first openly all-professional team in the world. The name often was shortened to the Reds, although team members were known as the Redlegs from 1954 to 1959 to forestall confusion with the communist movement. Today they're simply the Reds, the oldest team in Major League Baseball. That original team had an astonishing, 130-game winning streak.

Photo courtesy of the Library of Congress.

A series of small ballparks in the West End preceded League Park (initially called American Park), used until 1884. The team moved to League Park that year and played there until it burned in 1900. Games from 1902 to 1911 were at the Palace of the Fans, built on the League Park location.

In 1912, the team moved to Redland Field, later called Crosley Field, at Findlay and Western avenues in the West End. In 1919, it won the World Series against the Chicago White Sox, but the title was tainted by the "Black Sox Scandal," when it was learned that several Chicago players threw the championship in exchange for money from gamblers. On May 24, 1935, Crosley Field hosted the first Major League baseball game to be played under the lights.

Photo courtesy of baseballhall.com.

The Reds played at Crosley until 1970, when Riverfront Stadium opened. In the mid-1970s, the team was nicknamed "The Big Red Machine," with a powerhouse lineup that won back-to-back World Series titles in 1975 and 1976. Following a "wire-to-wire" 1990 season, in which the team remained in first place every day, the Reds won another World Series in a four-game sweep of the Oakland A's. Riverfront Stadium hosted baseball and football games, but the Reds and Bengals did not like sharing. Great American Ball Park opened in 2003 on a site just east of its predecessor. Within the stadium is an excellent Hall of Fame with museum-quality displays about the team's history.

Photo courtesy of Rick Pender.

Oldest Ice Cream Parlors

Graeter's
2704 Erie Ave., Hyde Park
graeters.com

Aglamesis Brothers
3046 Madison Rd., Oakley
aglamesis.com

At the age of 18, Louis C. Graeter (1852–1919) founded an ice cream company in 1870. The son of German immigrants, he opened a shop in Pendleton, a neighborhood in the east end of Over-the-Rhine. By 1883, he had several employees and two delivery wagons. He unexpectedly left town that year, but his brother Fred kept the business going. Louis returned around 1900 and with Regina Berger (1875–1955), his third wife, began to produce high-quality ice cream using two-gallon French pots, a small-batch process the company still uses. Following Louis's death in a 1919 streetcar accident, Regina expanded the business, opening shops in downtown Cincinnati and Hyde Park Square; the latter continues to operate in that historic location.

Today Graeter's is managed by the family's fourth generation, one of the most respected regional brands in America. It has 50 retail locations (18 in Cincinnati) selling premium ice cream, candy, and baked goods. It distributes ice

Photo courtesy of Rick Pender.

cream to 6,000 grocery stores nationwide. Locally, Graeter's outsells premium brands such as Ben & Jerry's and Häagen-Dazs, the only city in the United States where those brands are not top sellers. Chocolate chip flavors are the most popular, especially black raspberry chocolate chip, which constitutes 20 percent of Graeter's overall sales.

A smaller historic Cincinnati ice cream brand, Aglamesis Brothers, was established in 1908 by Greek immigrants. It's an esteemed competitor to Graeter's. The long, old-fashioned Aglamesis parlor, opened in 1913 on Oakley Square, continues to operate in its original location; ice cream and chocolates are made upstairs. Aglamesis is a go-to source for "opera cream" candies, a Cincinnati delicacy.

Graeter's combines flavor and cream into two-gallon stainless steel French Pots that are spun to -14 degrees Fahrenheit. Chocolate chips and other "inclusions" are added after 15–20 minutes. Ice cream is scooped by hand into pint containers — about 25,600 daily

----------1871

OLDEST LANDMARK AND PUBLIC SQUARE
FOUNTAIN SQUARE
Fifth and Vine Streets

W When Cincinnati's first settlers arrived, an Indian mound was located at the site of today's Fountain Square. Perhaps that magical earthen structure anticipated what would become downtown's symbolic center. But the arrival of the Tyler Davidson Fountain in October 1871 truly created a great gathering place. A gift to the city from hardware owner Henry Probasco (1820–1902) in memory of Davidson, his brother-in-law, the splendid fountain known as the Genius of Water replaced an unsightly butcher's market.

As business partners in 1860, Probasco and Davidson (1808–1865) considered donating a public fountain to the city; Davidson's unexpected death spurred Probasco to travel to Europe in search of a suitable memorial. He chose a design by sculptor

Photo courtesy of Rick Pender.

August von Kreling (1818–1876), and Munich's Royal Bronze Foundry did the casting. When first installed, the fountain was set on an elevated esplanade in the middle of Fifth Street between Vine and Walnut streets. Fountain Square has been remodeled and the fountain relocated several times, but it has remained the focal point.

With the inscription, "To the People of Cincinnati," on its base, the fountain is 38 feet tall. Water is its theme, celebrating the importance of the Ohio River to the city. The figure atop the fountain, the Genius of Water, is nine feet tall. Water rains down from her outstretched arms. Below her, the statue portrays benefits of water: steam, waterpower, navigation, and fisheries. Firefighters and farmers are represented, and playful children on fanciful drinking fountains featuring a dolphin, ducks, a snake, and a turtle. The fountain was made from 22 tons of cannon bronze, purchased from the Danish government.

For a century and a half, Fountain Square has drawn Cincinnatians to public celebrations, speeches, sports championships, concerts, and prayers and mourning. It's a daily gathering place for downtown workers.

The Tyler Davidson Fountain had a starring role in the opening credits for a 1978–1982 television series, WKRP in Cincinnati. The sitcom portrayed the misadventures of the staff at a struggling rock-and-roll radio station.

Oldest Hotels

The Cincinnatian Hotel

601 Vine St.
cincinnatianhotel.com

Hilton Cincinnati Netherland Plaza

Carew Tower, 35 W Fifth St.
historichotels.org/hotels-resorts/hilton-cincinnati-
netherland-plaza

Orchids at Palm Court Restaurant

orchidsatpalmcourt.com

W hen the Palace Hotel opened in 1882, it was considered "a grand hotel," featuring Second French Empire–style architecture. It had 300 rooms, and a shared bathroom at the end of each corridor. With electric lights and hydraulic elevators, it was considered a modern facility. Designed by Samuel Hannaford, the eight-story building was downtown Cincinnati's tallest building at the time.

In the mid-20th century, the Palace became The Cincinnatian Hotel. In 1980, it was listed on the National Register of Historic Places. It was attractively remodeled in 1987 to 167 guest suites, retaining the marble-and-walnut grand staircase in the imposing lobby.

Another downtown hotel, the Hilton Cincinnati Netherland Plaza, is significant historically and architecturally. Opened in 1931, it offered 800 rooms within the Carew Tower complex on Fifth Street between Vine and Race streets. A superb example of Art Deco architecture, it has numerous memorable spaces, including the Hall of Mirrors banquet room (inspired by the Palace of Versailles in France) and the gorgeously detailed Palm Court Bar with its esteemed Orchids Restaurant (awarded five diamonds by AAA). Some of this historic design was covered by modernization in the 1960s, but its 1930 murals and nickel-silver fixtures were restored authentically during a major facelift (1981–1983). Today, there are 561 guest rooms.

Over the years, guests at the Netherland have included Winston Churchill, Elvis Presley, Eleanor Roosevelt, Bing Crosby, and John and Jacqueline Kennedy. The hotel earned a National Historic Landmark designation in 1985.

The Carew Tower complex predates New York City's Rockefeller Center (opened in 1933), designed on a similar concept, combining an office tower, shops in an arcade, posh restaurants, and a glamorous hotel.

Palace Hotel, 1882. Photo courtesy of Cincinnati History Museum.

OLDEST CITY HALL
CINCINNATI CITY HALL
801 Plum St.
cincinnati-oh.gov/council/welcome-to-city-hall

N ot only is Cincinnati City Hall the region's oldest, it is cited generally as the greatest design by prolific architect **Samuel Hannaford**. It sits where the previous hall, a small, two-story building, was built in 1852. By the 1880s, Cincinnati was Ohio's largest city, requiring much more expansive quarters for elected officials and professional administrators. The old hall was demolished in 1888, and Hannaford was hired to design its replacement. The new City Hall was dedicated on May 13, 1893.

Built at a cost of $1.86 million, it's a textbook example of Richardsonian Romanesque architecture. Hannaford admired the ornamental style of H.H. Richardson (1838–1886), a New York architect whose massively arched and gabled buildings are found across the United States. Hannaford's design featured exterior banding with maroon sandstone. Arched windows exaggerate the impression of height by decreasing in size on successive upper floors. A nine-story rectangular clock tower rises 293 feet at the building's southeast corner.

Enormous stained glass windows at the Plum Street and Central Avenue entrances reflect the city's history, from Roman emperor Cincinnatus to Henry Wadsworth Longfellow's poem extolling "the Queen of the West." Inside are marble

Photo courtesy of Getty Images.

columns and stairways, illuminated by a stairwell skylight.
Wide corridors surround an open, central courtyard. City Hall
was listed on the National Register of Historic Places in 1972.
Situated near the **Plum Street Temple** and **St. Peter in Chains
Cathedral**, stately City Hall is the focal point of what has been
called "a remarkable architectural cluster."

The building has a large chamber for city council meetings.
Offices of the mayor and nine council members and their staffs
are within the building. Managing a 21st-century city today
requires considerably more space, so many departments are
housed in the buildings on Centennial Plaza on Central Avenue
behind City Hall.

*Architect Samuel Hannaford (1835–1911) was born in
Devonshire, England. His family came to southwest Ohio
in 1845. During his half-century career, he designed
numerous historic buildings, including Cincinnati
Music Hall (1878), the Palace Hotel (1882), and
waterworks structures in Eden Park (1883–1894).*

OLDEST JEWELRY STORE
THE RICHTER & PHILLIPS COMPANY

601 Main St.
richterphillips.com

I t was 1896 when Edward Richter and the three Phillips brothers opened their downtown Cincinnati jewelry store and produced a mail-order catalog for customers nationwide. The Richter & Phillips Company met with considerable success but struggled during the Depression; Frederick W. Fehr, a traveling diamond salesman for a different company, took out a loan to keep the store open. He bought out the remaining stockholders in 1930.

Fehr retired in 1972 at the age of 90. His son, Fred Fehr Jr., began to work for the company when he was 12 or 13 years old, loading and unloading trucks. Fred Fehr's son, Rick (Frederick Fehr III), left the company after college but returned in 1981 as a graduate gemologist responsible for diamond and gemstone purchasing and sales. His

Photo courtesy of Rick Pender.

brother, Art, also became a graduate gemologist and joined the business in 1990.

This truly family-owned business has been committed to its downtown Cincinnati location since it began. For many years, it operated in the Temple Bar Building at Court and Main streets near the Hamilton County Courthouse. It moved to the ground floor of the Gwynn Building on Sixth Street in 1977. In 2016, the Richter & Phillips Company purchased and relocated to the opposite corner of Sixth and Main streets, a one-time bank building with a basement vault and more recently an entertainment venue. The company is known for its stunning corner showroom, where beautiful jewelry and watches are on display.

OLDEST SKYSCRAPERS
INGALLS BUILDING
6 E 4th St.

PNC TOWER (OFFICIALLY THE 4TH & VINE TOWER)
1 W 4th St.

Years before the Carew Tower became downtown Cincinnati's best-known skyscraper, a daring 15-story, 210-foot building dominated the skyline. The Ingalls Building was a reinforced-concrete structure that had many skeptics shaking their heads when it went up and up in 1903. A doubting journalist camped out nearby when construction was completed, waiting for it to fall.

Cincinnati architects Alfred Elzner (1862–1933) and George Anderson (1869–1916) designed the structure with eight-inch-thick exterior walls made from 16-foot square slabs, reinforced with steel rods, or rebar. Its successful construction contributed to the acceptance of concrete construction in high-rise buildings, adding to fire resistance and noise dampening. The first three stories are covered with white marble; the next 11 stories have glazed gray brick; the top floor and cornice have glazed white terra cotta. It was named for businessman Melville Ezra Ingalls (1842–1914), a railroad tycoon and respected philanthropist who devoted significant support to the **Cincinnati Art Museum**. Now a 126-room Courtyard by Marriott Hotel, it continues to stand at Fourth and Vine streets, the city's oldest skyscraper.

Nearby and also predating the Carew Tower was the headquarters of the Union Central Life Insurance building (1913), designed by renowned architect Cass Gilbert (1849–1934). An Ohio native, he is most remembered for his design of the US Supreme Court building. His Cincinnati masterpiece is today's PNC Tower. When the 31-story building was completed, it was the tallest building outside New York City.

The 15-story Ingalls Building (below, left) was truly America's first skyscraper in 1903. The 31-story PNC Tower (below, right), built in 1913 as the headquarters of an insurance company, was at the time the tallest building west of New York City

---

PNC Tower. Photo courtesy of Cincinnati Convention & Visitors Bureau.

Ingalls Building. Photo courtesy of Cincinnati History Museum.

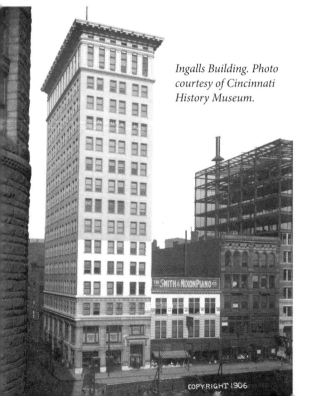

OLDEST HAT SHOP
BATSAKES HAT SHOP
1 W 6th St.

George and Pete Batsakes opened their hat shop at Sixth and Walnut streets in 1907. It's Cincinnati's oldest—and truly the only—place to shop for personally tailored hats. Since 1973, it's been owned and operated by George and Pete's nephew, Gus Miller (1934), who arrived from Greece in 1951. His uncles put him to work sweeping floors the day after he showed up in Cincinnati. Before too long, he learned to make everything from fedoras to straw hats, most of which take three to five hours by hand.

Photo courtesy of Rick Pender.

Customers come from near and far. During his seven decades working at Batsakes, Miller's most famous and beloved client has been opera star Luciano Pavarotti (1935–2007), whose recordings provide daily background music for the shop that's been located at Sixth and Vine since 2001. (It previously sat at Sixth and Walnut streets, where the Contemporary Arts Center now is situated.) Miller also provided hats for three presidents (Reagan and both Bushes), singers Tony Bennett and Bob Dylan, and legendary Bengals football coach Paul Brown. Customer service is his byword, and he relies on word of mouth to sustain his business.

Oldest Italian Restaurants
Scotti's Italian Restaurant
919 Vine St.

Pompilio's
600 Washington Ave., Newport, KY
pompilios.com

I t's unusual for a restaurant to last for more than a century, especially under the ownership of the same family. Scotti's Italian Restaurant and its owners, the DiMarcos and Scoleris, reached that milestone in 2012. In 1912, Concetta and Salvatore Scoleri started to serve Italian fare in downtown Cincinnati. In 1953, they settled into Scotti's current home on Vine Street.

The Scoleris and Concetta's mother, Terese Saltera, came to Cincinnati from Philadelphia, where they ran the European Hotel. They named their Cincinnati restaurant for Antonio Scotti, a singer with New York City's Metropolitan Opera, whom they met in Pennsylvania. Diners today still hear opera music on the sound system. In the 21st century, the establishment is run by the DiMarco siblings, Marco, Pat, and Rina, the Scoleris' great-grandchildren.

Scotti's traditional red-sauce and garlic cuisine reflects the family's roots in Calabria, a city on Italy's southern tip. Once upon a time, diners were scolded for cutting spaghetti with a

table knife. The décor of the downstairs dining room features Chianti bottles on the ceiling, lots of historic family photos, and walls embedded with multicolored tile.

The honors for longtime Italian dining in Northern Kentucky go to Pompilio's in Newport, which opened in 1933 as Pompilio House, a name shortened in the 1940s. Its Washington Avenue address dates to 1902, when Kettenacker's Saloon was a bar closely affiliated with the nearby **George Wiedemann Brewing Company**. Pompilio's earned a moment of fame in the 1988 Academy Award–winning film *Rain Man*: the autistic central character played by Dustin Hoffman dropped toothpicks on the floor, and immediately announced how many there were.

While Cincinnati and Northern Kentucky are thoroughly German, enclaves of Italian immigrants settled on both sides of the river. Newport, Kentucky, annually celebrates that history with Italianfest in June, featuring food and music on the riverfront.

Oldest Children's Theatre

Children's Theatre of Cincinnati
4015 Red Bank Rd.
thechildrenstheatre.com

The Taft Theatre
317 E 5th St.
tafttheatre.org

Since 1919, the Children's Theatre of Cincinnati (TCT) has introduced young audiences to live theater, making it the oldest theater of its kind not just in Cincinnati, but in the United States. It began with Helen Schuster-Martin and her School of Drama. Active in the Junior League of Cincinnati, she used her expertise to direct the first production for young audiences by The Junior League Players; an early show was a stage version of *The Wizard of Oz*. The League continued to manage TCT's operations until 1947, when it became an independent, nonprofit organization.

After a season at Hughes High School, the company moved to Over-the-Rhine's Emery Theatre,

Photo courtesy of the Children's Theatre of Cincinnati.

where it presented shows for two decades. In 1969, productions for school audiences moved to the Taft Theatre. In 1982, public performances at the Taft were added to each show. The 21st century schedule typically includes four productions per season, especially "junior" versions of musicals—shortened to match young audience members' attention spans. In 2010, the TCT Academy began to offer classes for youngsters.

In 2015, TCT moved its administrative offices to a former warehouse facility on Red Bank Road near Fairfax, complete with a small performance space, costume shop, and studios for various Academy classes, as well as offices for the professional staff. With continued growth, TCT routinely serves more than 100,000 children and families annually on the mainstage, and more than 80,000 with touring productions.

The Children's Theatre has been the first live theater experience for area youngsters for more than a century. School buses deliver thousands of kids for the company's annual productions.

OLDEST ART DECO BUILDINGS

DIXIE TERMINAL
49 E 4th St.

CAREW TOWER
441 Vine St.

Cincinnati is a treasure trove of glamorous Art Deco architecture, typified by geometrical forms and low-relief decorative panels. The style was popular in the 1920s and 1930s for local buildings, many of which still are beautifully present.

The area's oldest transportation terminal, the 10-story Dixie Terminal (1921) at Fourth and Walnut streets, served streetcars and buses crossing the Roebling Suspension Bridge to and from Kentucky. Its office building was home to the Cincinnati Stock Exchange and the Cincinnati Street Railway Exchange.

Designed by Cincinnati architect Frederick W. Garber, its Art Deco details include a barrel-vaulted arcade and an ornate, two-story atrium. The entry features a **Rookwood Pottery** tile frame.

Photo courtesy of Hilton Cincinnati Netherland Plaza.

Photo courtesy of Hilton Cincinnati Netherland Plaza.

For many years, the 49-story Carew Tower (1930) was downtown's tallest building, at 574 feet. Featuring an office tower, a department store, a two-story shopping arcade, and the elegant Netherland Plaza Hotel, the complex predated New York City's Rockefeller Center (1933) as "a city within a city." Designed by the Chicago firm W.W. Ahlschlager & Associates, it was built in 1930 by the same construction company that erected New York's Empire State Building.

The Netherland Hotel was the brainchild of real estate developer John J. Emery Jr. (1898–1976). Several banks turned him down in 1929 for funding to build the complex, so, fortuitously, he sold his personal stock fortune just before the market crashed. The Carew Tower is full of lavish Art Deco details: metalwork and grillwork in elevators and lighting fixtures, **Rookwood Pottery** tiles, marble finishes, sculptures by Rene Paul Chamberlain (1893–1955), and numerous original murals by Louis Grell (1887–1960). The ornate Hall of Mirrors banquet room was inspired by the Palace of Versailles in France.

Cincinnati Union Terminal (1931) and the *Cincinnati Times-Star* building (1933) are discussed elsewhere.

Oldest Chili Parlors

Empress Chili
7934 Alexandria Pike, Alexandria, KY
empresschilialexandria.com

Dixie Chili & Deli
733 Monmouth Ave., Newport, KY
dixiechili.com

Camp Washington Chili
3004 Colerain Ave.
campwashingtonchili.com

Skyline Chili, Inc.
Many locations
skylinechili.com

Gold Star Chili, Inc.
Many locations
goldstarchili.com

Cincinnati's unique, local style of chili features finely ground and specially seasoned meat sauce served over thin spaghetti and topped with cheddar cheese. (It also tops hot dogs, called "coneys.") Chili providers keep their specific recipes top secret. But it's commonly agreed that they include cinnamon, nutmeg, allspice, clove, cumin, chili powder, bay leaf, and sometimes dark chocolate.

It's the creation of Macedonian immigrants from northern

Photo courtesy of Rick Pender.

Greece. The first of them, Tom and John Kiradjieff, launched Empress Chili in a tiny downtown eatery in 1922 next door to the Empress Burlesque Theater. (Their parlor now is located in Alexandria, Kentucky.) Nicholas Sarakatsannis worked briefly for Empress before he started Dixie Chili in Newport in 1929; it's still there, with two more Kentucky locations in Erlanger and Covington.

The best-known chili brand is Skyline, with locations across Ohio, Indiana, Kentucky—and Florida! It was launched by Nicholas Lambrinides in 1949 with a parlor atop Price Hill that has a spectacular view of the city's skyline, thus the brand's name. Gold Star (1965) was launched by four Daoud brothers from Jordan. Its many locations feature broader menus, including burgers and sandwiches.

Independent parlors can be found across the region. Camp Washington Chili (1940), founded by Johnny Johnson (born Ioannis Ioannoy), is the oldest, most often cited by national media.

Photo courtesy of Joan Kaup.

OLDEST NEWSPAPER BUILDINGS

FORMER *CINCINNATI ENQUIRER* BUILDING
617 Vine Street

The *Cincinnati Enquirer* was first published on April 10, 1841, reporting the death of President William Henry Harrison six days earlier. Among the first papers to produce a Sunday edition (1848), it's now the oldest Sunday newspaper in the nation. After a fire in 1866, it moved to 617 Vine St., its address for 126 years as "the Grand Old Lady of Vine Street." With a mix of architectural styles from 1927, featuring a beautiful marble lobby with bronze ornamentation and a brass sculpture, the building was placed on the National Register of Historic Places in 1985. In 1992, the Enquirer moved to a new office building at 312 Elm St. The Enquirer's ghostly title remains above the doors to a building now housing two suite hotels, a Hampton Inn and a Homewood Suites.

Cincinnati's longtime afternoon newspaper, the *Cincinnati Post*, started in 1881; its Northern Kentucky edition began in 1890, the *Kentucky Post*. Another paper,

Photo courtesy of Cincinnati History Museum.

Photo courtesy of Rick Pender.

the *Times-Star*, had been created in 1880 when **Charles Phelps Taft** merged two popular publications, *Spirit of the Times* and the *Evening Star*. The *Times-Star*'s glorious 1933 Art Deco tower at 800 Broadway was designed by Eldridge Hannaford (1892-1975), son of architect **Samuel Hannaford**. Its facades feature reliefs of giant allegorical figures representing pioneers of printing (Thomas Caxton, Johannes Gutenberg, and Ben Franklin) as well as the essential qualities of a newspaper: Truth, Speed, Patriotism, and Progress.

In 1958, the *Post*'s owner, Scripps-Howard Newspapers, acquired the *Times-Star* and merged the two papers. After 30 years in a joint operating agreement with the *Enquirer*, the *Post* ceased publication in 2007. Today, 800 Broadway is an office building for employees of several Hamilton County departments. The building was placed on the National Register of Historic Places in 1983.

The Cincinnati *and* Kentucky Post *newspapers were sustained between 1977 and 2007 by a joint operating agreement with the* Cincinnati Enquirer. *When the JOA ended, the* Post, *an afternoon newspaper, ceased publication.*

OLDEST MOVIE PALACE REMNANTS

THE MIGHTY WURLITZER

1241 Elm St., Over-the-Rhine
friendsofmusichall.org/events/concerts-with-the-mighty-
wurlitzer-organ/

DUKE ENERGY CONVENTION CENTER

525 Elm St.
duke-energycenter.com

Cincinnati's movie palaces all have been demolished, but they are not forgotten. The first to open was the Palace Theatre (16 E 6th St.) on December 6, 1919. It began as a live performance venue, but also served as a movie theater. Its Italianate architecture won recognition as a historic site, but that did not forestall demolition in late 1982. It was replaced by an office building.

Photo courtesy of Friends of Music Hall.

The Shubert Theatre (90 E 7th St.) opened on September 25, 1921. Its 3,000-seat auditorium was inside an 1848 building, the city's original YMCA facility. Movies were screened there until 1953, when it became the Reverend Earl Ivies's Revival Temple. Two years later, movies returned. It closed permanently in 1975 and became a parking lot a year later, then eventually the site for another office building.

The 3,000-seat E. F. Albee Photoplays Theatre (12 E 5th St.) opened on Christmas Eve 1927 with Clara Bow in *Get Your Man* plus five vaudeville acts. It soon became known as the RKO Albee. It was demolished in 1977 to make way for the Westin Hotel. (Historic photos of the Albee can be viewed on the hotel's second-floor atrium balcony.)

The Albee's front façade, a massive arch supported by four pillars, was preserved and incorporated into the Fifth Street façade of the Cincinnati Convention Center. It's the oldest remnant of those glorious theaters. One more reminder of the Albee's grandeur remains: its Mighty Wurlitzer theater organ from 1927. In the 1960s, it was donated to the Emery Theatre (1112 Walnut St., Over-the-Rhine) where it was used occasionally until 1999, when it was put into storage. In 2007, it was fully restored and installed in **Cincinnati Music Hall**'s ballroom. It's still played there for silent movies and holiday celebrations.

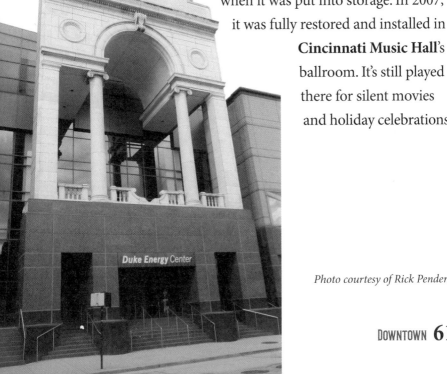

Photo courtesy of Rick Pender.

Oldest Modern Art Museum
Lois & Richard Rosenthal Center for Contemporary Art
44 E 6th St.
contemporaryartscenter.org

I t might seem strange to include a modern art museum among Cincinnati's oldest institutions, but definitely the Contemporary Arts Center qualifies. It began as the Modern Art Society in 1939, founded by Betty Pollak Rauh (1915–2001), Peggy Frank Crawford (1917–2015), and Rita Rentschler Cushman (1914–1994), three young women who raised funds to give modern art its first home in the lower levels of the Cincinnati

Photo courtesy of Getty Images.

Art Museum. Its name changed in 1952, but the CAC's non-collecting purpose was steadfast, focused on showcasing "the art of the last five minutes."

After several temporary locations, it moved in 1964 into the Mercantile Center on Fifth Street. Among the 400 exhibitions presented during its three decades at that address, the most remembered was "The Perfect Moment" (1990), featuring controversial photos by Robert Mapplethorpe that led to charges of pandering obscenity, the first trial resulting from an exhibition at an American art museum. The final verdict: Not guilty on all charges.

In 2003, the CAC moved to a new facility of its own with 80,000 square feet of exhibition space. It was designed by Zaha Hadid (1950–2016), the first American museum to be envisioned by a female architect. A slightly askew stack of boxes, it is its own work of modern art. The *New York Times* called it "the best new building since the Cold War."

With exhibitions of new work in painting, sculpture, photography, architecture, performance art, and new media, the CAC has presented work by many renowned artists early in their careers, including pop artist Andy Warhol (1928–1987).

The three women who started the Contemporary Arts Center were advised by Edward M. M. Warburg, who founded New York City's Museum of Modern Art and the American Ballet.

OLDEST MURALS
ALLEGRO
37 W 7th St.

ARTWORKS CINCINNATI
20 E Central Pkwy.
artworkscincinnati.org

In the early 1970s, 10 Cincinnati artists and designers were commissioned to create large designs to mask the damage done by urban renewal a decade earlier. The project, organized by gallery owner Carl Solway and his assistant, Jack Boulton, was called "Urban Walls." Only one mural survives today, downtown on West Seventh Street. Barron Krody's geometric piece, *Allegro*, features strips of vibrant yellow and green emanating from an abstract orange base. Krody's award-winning graphic design was featured on the poster that announced the project.

Murals are more commonplace today in downtown and beyond, thanks to ArtWorks Cincinnati, founded in 1996. Over the years, it has provided thousands of youth, ages 14 to 21, the opportunity—as summer

Barron Krody's Allegro.
Photo courtesy of Rick Pender.

At 12th and Jackson Streets, Kim Krause's "Energy & Grace." Photo courtesy of Rick Pender.

employees—to work on creating public and private art projects designed by professional artists. Today 200 permanent outdoor murals grace walls throughout the region, including more than 40 in the city core. One of the oldest, *The Face of the Arts* (1100 Race St.), was painted in 2007. Perhaps the most spectacular is *Martha, the Last Passenger Pigeon* (2013, 15 E Eighth St.), based on a painting by legendary wildlife artist John Ruthven (1927–2020). One of ArtWorks' largest creations, it represents the last survivor of a species: Martha died in 1914 at the **Cincinnati Zoo**. ArtWorks's murals have contributed to Greater Cincinnati's reputation as an arts destination.

ArtWorks tour guides—some teens, some older volunteers—offer a variety of public walking tour options to view spectacular murals throughout Downtown Cincinnati from May through October.

OVER-THE-RHINE

OLDEST CANAL
CANAL MUSEUM
16 N Verity Pkwy., Middletown, OH
middletownhistoricalsociety.com/canal-museum

S hortly after Ohio became a state in 1803, its General
Assembly took up the issue of canals. Surveying was
undertaken in 1820, and in 1825 construction began on
the first leg of the Miami and Erie Canal, using a path conceived
by **Dr. Daniel Drake**. By 1828, a 66-mile stretch connected
Dayton and Cincinnati. The canal linking Lake Erie to the
Ohio River was completed in 1845. Although the towboats
were slow, by 1831 more than 7,000 passengers had traveled
between Dayton and Cincinnati. The canal entered Cincinnati
at Lockland and followed a 12-mile flat stretch, concluding with
today's Central Parkway and Eggleston Avenue before reaching
the Ohio River.

In the city, the canal was traversed by small bridges. The
densely German neighborhood north of downtown came to be
called Over-the-Rhine, as if the narrow canal was Cincinnati's
version of Bavaria's Rhine River. Although initially a joke, the
name stuck.

By the 1870s, railroads rapidly took over freight
transportation, and the canal fell into disuse. Flooding in 1913
spelled its demise; by the 1920s it was no longer in use. Its
unsightly and unsanitary downtown stretch was paved over in
1920, only to be dug up again shortly for a never-completed

subway system. Repaved in 1928, it became Central Parkway.

Middletown's Canal Museum is a replica of an 1842 lock tender's house. The canal's groundbreaking took place in that city on July 21, 1825. **Washington Platform Saloon & Restaurant** on the south edge of Over-the-Rhine began as Johan Armleder Wine & Lager Beer Saloon in 1870, a lively spot frequented by residents of Over-the-Rhine and a frequent stop for canal travelers. Its Canal Room is a showcase of historic photos.

Dr. Daniel Drake (1785–1852) earned the first medical diploma granted to anyone west of the Allegheny Mountains. A renaissance man from Kentucky, he came to Cincinnati in 1807 to practice medicine, but he was involved in countless early advancements, including the canal.

Photo courtesy of onlyinyourstate.com.

Oldest Brewery Buildings

Throughout the Over-the-Rhine Neighborhood

brewingheritagetrail.org
americanlegacytours.com

Cincinnati's first British brewers produced ales. When German immigrants arrived in the mid-19th century, the brewing industry expanded and changed, producing lighter, golden brews called lagers. At least three dozen breweries were operating by 1860, most in the Over-the-Rhine neighborhood. Around 1900, local citizens individually drank 58 gallons per year, when the national per capita average was just over 16 gallons. Late in the 1800s, there were 3,400 drinking establishments in the city, one bar for every 20 registered voters. Many were tied specifically to one of the larger breweries.

Nationwide Prohibition by the 18th Amendment to the US Constitution started in 1919 with the enforcement of the Volstead Act. A few breweries retooled to soft drinks or near-beers, but Prohibition spelled the end for most of them. The 21st-century renaissance of craft brewing has resurrected several breweries' names and original buildings.

George Schmelzer, a German immigrant, opened the Andrew Jackson Brewery in 1829, Over-the-Rhine's first brewery (208 Mohawk St.). Its name honored America's seventh president, elected that year. In 1855, its name changed to the Jackson

Brewery. By 1885, it had 62 employees and was producing 100,000 barrels annually. It lasted until 1941. For nearly 50 years, the Cincinnati Metal Blast Company used the building as a warehouse; its name, painted on

Jackson Brewery, 1829.
Photo courtesy of Rick Pender.

the building's crown, clearly is visible where the brewery's logo was originally displayed.

In 1845 German immigrants Johann Sohn (1817–1876) and George Klotter (1805–1883) launched the Hamilton Brewery (244–246 W McMicken Ave.). Cool beer was stored in lagering tunnels dug into the hillside. In 1907, it became the Mohawk Brewing Co. During Prohibition, a raid by federal agents revealed 100 barrels of illegal beer, and the operation was closed. From the end of Prohibition until its closing in 1957, it was the Clyffside Brewery and later the Red Top Brewery. In 2020, the building was reborn with the old Clyffside Brewery name, with plans for event spaces featuring bars, catering kitchens, and decks.

German immigrant **Christian Moerlein** (1818–1897) began his brewing operations modestly in 1853, and is another legendary brewery name that's present today.

In 1885, Louis Hudepohl (1842–1902), Cincinnati's first American-born beer baron, established Hudepohl Brewery (40 E McMicken Ave.). For many years, the brewery's highly visible smokestack stood at its Queensgate facility. Brewing stopped in 1988; the stack and other brewery buildings were demolished in 2019.

The Vine Street Brewery (1622 Vine Street) was owned by German-born John Kauffman (1830–1886). Launched in 1859, it became the Kauffman Brewing Company and by 1870 was brewing 50,000 barrels a year. Today it's the Guild Haus loft apartment building. The Kauffman malt house (1621 Moore St.) and underground lager cellars have become the latter-day Christian Moerlein Brewery, with a gallery of Moerlein artifacts.

The Bellevue Brewery's 1866 building (603 W McMicken Ave.) has an entrance at 2260 Central Parkway that's familiar to music fans as "the Mockbee," since musical events were presented in its lagering tunnels in the 1990s and early 2000s. The Bellevue Brewery was operated by George Klotter (1805–1882), and by his sons until Prohibition.

Beer brewing also flourished in Northern Kentucky: Bavarian Brewery in Covington began in 1859 on Pike Street, producing more than 200,000 barrels annually in the early 20th century. Today, the building houses offices for Kenton County

Today's Rhinegeist Brewery building was built by Christian Moerlein in the 19th century. Photo courtesy of Rick Pender.

Fiscal Court. The large brewery established in Newport in 1870 by George Wiedemann (1833–1890), eventually became an ornate, five-acre complex at Sixth and Columbia streets, designed by **Samuel Hannaford**. It produced approximately 100,000 barrels annually in the 1890s. During Prohibition it operated illegally in partnership with bootlegger George Remus (1874–1952), selling millions of gallons of beer until federal authorities shut it down in 1927. The brand was resurrected in the 21st century with facilities in the Cincinnati neighborhood of St. Bernard.

OLDEST CHURCH

OLD ST. MARY'S ROMAN CATHOLIC CHURCH

123 E 13th St., Over-the-Rhine
oldstmarys.org

CHRIST CHURCH CATHEDRAL

318 E 4th St.
cincinnaticathedral.com

COVENANT-FIRST PRESBYTERIAN CHURCH

717 Elm St.
covfirstchurch.org

Cincinnati's oldest church building is Over-the-Rhine's Old St. Mary's. The cornerstone for "St. Marien's Kirche" was laid in 1841 with inscriptions in German, English, and Latin. Built from bricks that women baked in their ovens, its first service was on July 3, 1842. Masses still are conducted in Latin, English, and German. The steeple contains the city's oldest clock tower, containing the first bell installed by the Verdin Bell Company. A 1996 renovation brought the building back to its original beauty.

Several Protestant congregations formed in Cincinnati's early days. The Reverend James Kemper (1753–1834) gathered Presbyterian worshipers in 1790 in his Walnut Hills log cabin, now found at Heritage Village Museum at Sharon Woods. Second Presbyterian Church branched off in 1816. The Reverend Lyman Beecher, Harriet Beecher Stowe's father, had a contentious term as pastor there (1833–1843). In 1875, that congregation moved to a Gothic-style structure at the east end of Piatt Park. Covenant-First Presbyterian Church resulted from a 1933 merger of six downtown churches.

The Episcopalian Parish of Christ Church first met in Dr. Daniel Drake's Third Street home on May 18, 1817. Original members included General William Henry Harrison, the ninth president of the United States; General Arthur St. Clair Jr, first governor of the Northwest Territory; and James Taylor, founder of Newport, Kentucky. Early worshipers later gathered in a cotton factory and a former Baptist meeting house before moving in 1835 to a permanent downtown address, a red-brick, Gothic-style church with octagonal towers and pinnacles. In 1909, a parish house was added with funds from Mary Emery (1844–1927), who envisioned it as a nonsectarian community center serving church members and poor, working-class people. The original 1835 church was demolished in 1955 to make way for a more modern structure, dedicated in 1957.

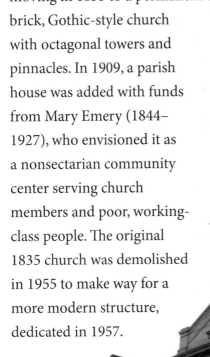

Photo courtesy of Rick Pender.

Oldest Bell & Clock Maker

The Verdin Company

444 Reading Rd.
verdin.com

I n 1835, brothers Francis and Michael Verdin immigrated to the United States from Alsace in France. They partnered with iron-forging and clock-making skills to begin a clock business. The Verdin Company became a world-renowned family manufacturer, a pioneer and innovator of cast bronze bells, carillons, clocks, towers, and organs. Their first installation in 1842 was clock and bell equipment still in use at **Old St. Mary's** in Over-the-Rhine.

Today, Verdin Bell is managed by the sixth generation of ownership, making it one of the nation's oldest family-owned manufacturers. Current products include bells, bell equipment, restoration, digital carillons, and clocks. The company has a history of more than 55,000 installations in churches, universities, and town halls across America. In 1998 and 1999 it oversaw the casting and installation in Newport, Kentucky, of the largest swinging cast bell in America, the 33-ton World Peace Bell.

The company is headquartered in the desanctified but still beautiful St. Paul's Church (1850) in Cincinnati's Pendleton neighborhood.

Photo courtesy of Rick Pender.

Oldest Butchers

Eckerlin Meats
116 W Elder St., Findlay Market
eckerlinmeats.com

Avril-Bleh & Sons Meat Market & Deli
33 E Court St.
avril-blehmeats.com

Freestanding butcher shops are a rarity in the 21st century. But Cincinnati has two that qualify as legendary. In 1852 Ernie Eckerlin, an immigrant from Baden, Germany, launched a Cincinnati slaughterhouse. When Findlay Market began in 1855, he opened a retail stand there managed by his daughter Frieda. She married a fellow employee, Al Lillis. Today the fifth and sixth generations of Eckerlin-Lillis descendants run the business.

Goetta is a uniquely Cincinnati favorite, a fried patty of ground pork and beef, oatmeal, onions, and spices. "Eckerlin's Best Goetta" is the shop's most popular product, selling 300 to 500 pounds weekly. Customers also come for fresh cuts of beef, pork, and chicken (especially stuffed chicken breasts), plus sausages, bacon, and even bison.

Another longtime destination for Cincinnati carnivores, Avril-Bleh & Sons Meat Market & Deli, opened more than a century ago in 1894. Anton Avril (1862–1926) was the founder; its ownership also passed through several generations until 1998, when Len Bleh bought the business.

Photo courtesy of Rick Pender.

Avril-Bleh is known for its array of sausages, including bratwursts and mettwursts, locally called "brats" and "metts," and hot dogs. The shop also offers steaks, briskets, pork roasts, ribs, cold cuts, ground meat, plus domestic and imported cheeses. Summertime meat sales average 3,000 pounds weekly and even more during the holidays. When the weather is nice, lunchtime fare is available hot off a grill on the Court Street sidewalk to be enjoyed at tables there.

Goetta is so popular locally that there are not one but two annual summertime goetta festivals. Attendees can sample goetta served in many imaginative ways, from loaded tater tots and nachos to sliders, cheese coneys, and more.

Oldest Public Market

Findlay Market

1801 Race St., Over-the-Rhine
findlaymarket.org

C incinnati once had nine walkable public markets serving downtown neighborhoods. Within walking distance, food could be purchased daily from butchers and fish sellers, produce vendors and farmers. Just one has survived: Findlay Market is, in fact, the oldest public market in Ohio.

General James Findlay (1770–1835) was a veteran of the War of 1812 and twice served as Cincinnati's mayor (1805, 1810). He parlayed his success as a merchant into land acquisition, especially property in the Northern Liberties, a densely wooded area just beyond the city limits. He planned to establish a market in an open area in the midst of "Findlay's Woods," but died before it was created. His heirs donated the site for a market and named it for him. The open-sided pavilion was ready for business in 1855.

Photo courtesy of Liz Dufour.

Photo courtesy of CincinnatiUSA.com.

Early in the 20th century, Findlay Market was enclosed for health reasons; plumbing and refrigeration were added. Throughout the century, it grew as a mecca for shoppers, politicians, tourists, and entrepreneurial merchants. Starting in 1920, an annual parade sponsored by the merchants celebrated baseball's opening day and the **Cincinnati Reds**, baseball's first professional team. Units and bands began at the market and marched to the ballpark of the moment—Crosley Field (until 1970), Riverfront Stadium (1970–2002), or Great American Ball Park (starting in 2003).

Today visitors can find boutique shops, restaurants, a beer garden, and lots of fresh food in the market building and the adjacent neighborhood. In 2019, *Newsweek* named it one of the 10 best food markets in the world, the only one in the United States so designated. It was entered on the National Register of Historic Places in 1972.

Numerous Findlay Market vendors have long histories, some going back five or six generations. Shoppers flock to the market on Saturday mornings, but the varied fare can be perused and purchased Tuesday through Sunday.

Oldest Beer

Christian Moerlein Lager House
115 Joe Nuxhall Way,
Smale Riverfront Park
moerleinlagerhouse.com

Christian Moerlein Malt House Tap Room
1621 Moore St., Over-the-Rhine

Rhinegeist Brewery
1910 Elm St., Over-the-Rhine
rhinegeist.com

The influx of beer-drinking Germans in the 19th century created a demand for crisp, pale lagers that became the popular products of Cincinnati breweries. The leading producer was Christian Moerlein (1818–1897), an immigrant who began his brewing operations modestly in 1853 on Elm Street.

When he first came to Cincinnati, Moerlein's business was an Elm Street blacksmith shop; he lived nearby. He sold it and launched a brewery that he operated, eventually with his sons, George and John. By 1855, they were producing 2,000 barrels annually, and by 1859 that volume doubled. For the latter decades of the 19th century, Moerlein was the city's leading brewery. Like many others, it closed with the onset of Prohibition, tried a comeback in the 1930s, but officially dissolved in 1934.

Photo courtesy of cincymuseum.org.

That wasn't the end of the city's oldest, most legendary beer. In 1981 the Hudepohl Brewing Company resurrected the label and began brewing a select lager that became the first and only American beer to be recognized with Germany's *Rhineheitsgebot* purity designation, a regulation that limited the ingredients to water, barley, and hops. It was a popular brand, but as Hudepohl merged and faded, Christian Moerlein almost disappeared again.

In 2004, Greg Hardaman, a Cincinnati beer industry veteran, purchased an array of brands and recipes and launched a new Christian Moerlein Brewing Company. (He resurrected other historic brands including Schoenlein's Little Kings Cream Ale and several of Hudepohl's popular brews.) Cincinnati's oldest beer again was available. Dubbed "the beer that built Cincinnati," Christian Moerlein is featured on tap at Hardaman's popular Moerlein Lager House, west of Great American Ballpark on Cincinnati's riverfront, as well as at a tap room in Over-the-Rhine.

The popular Rhinegeist Brewery operates in a building that was originally the 19th-century packaging and bottling plant for Moerlein's brewery.

Photo courtesy of Rick Pender.

───────────────────────────────1867

OLDEST MUSIC SCHOOL
UNIVERSITY OF CINCINNATI'S COLLEGE CONSERVATORY OF MUSIC

W Corry St. at Jefferson Ave., Clifton
uc.ccm.edu

Cincinnati's oldest music school, the University of Cincinnati's
College-Conservatory of Music, accrued its history from
two prior institutions. The Cincinnati Conservatory of
Music was the city's first music school, founded in 1867 by Clara
Baur. It was part of Miss Nourse's School for Young Ladies on
Park Avenue in Walnut Hills, where Baur offered classes in
voice and piano. In 1878, George Ward Nichols founded the
College of Music with support from Reuben Springer, the great
philanthropist of **Cincinnati Music Hall**, built in the same year

Photo courtesy of UC/CCM.

just north of the college's campus. (Nichols and his wife, **Maria Longworth Nichols**, were major arts supporters.) Theodore Thomas (1835–1905), a legendary conductor, was recruited as the college's first director; in 1895 he became the first conductor of the **Cincinnati Symphony Orchestra**.

Photo courtesy of UC/CCM.

The College and the Conservatory merged in 1955 and subsequently were absorbed into UC in 1962, where the division's hyphenated name typically is shortened to CCM. Today, it's one of the most respected professional training programs in the United States for music, voice, dance, theater (its renowned musical theater program is the oldest in the United States), electronic media, and arts administration, with an enrollment of approximately 1,500; students come from 43 different US states and 32 foreign countries.

The only building remaining from the College of Music (1228 Central Parkway) is the headquarters of the Pipe Fitters Union Local #392. Its musical roots are evident in the reliefs of cherubs and legendary composers on the façade above the entrance, likely created at Maria Longworth's **Rookwood Pottery**.

Photo courtesy of UC/CCM.

OLDEST ART SCHOOL
ART ACADEMY OF CINCINNATI
1212 Jackson St., Over-the-Rhine
artacademy.edu

Cincinnati's oldest art school was established as the McMicken School of Design in 1869, a department of the University of Cincinnati. In 1884, it became the Art Academy of Cincinnati (AAC), the museum school of the **Cincinnati Art Museum**, with classrooms, studios, and offices in a building adjacent to the museum. As enrollment grew, it also had classes in a converted school building in the Mount Adams neighborhood. In 1998, the Art Academy separated from the museum to become an independent college of art and design. In 2005, AAC moved to Over-the-Rhine, adapting a pair of converted warehouse buildings into classrooms, studios, and offices. It played a pivotal role in that neighborhood's evolution into a thriving arts district.

Several noteworthy artists trained at the Art Academy. Renowned painter Frank Duveneck (1848–1919) returned in the 1890s to teach and became the school's leader. Other respected graduates were Elizabeth Nourse (1859–1938), a respected painter of peasant women; Charley Harper (1922–2007), whose wildlife-inspired modernist images are well-known; realistic wildlife painter John Ruthven (1927); and Tom Wesselman (1931-2004), a noted pop artist. Julian Stanczak

Photo courtesy of the Cincinnati Enquirer *Archives.*

(1928–2017), founder of the Op Art movement, taught at AAC from 1957 to 1964.

Maria Longworth Nichols (1849–1932) enrolled in a course in china painting at the Art Academy of Cincinnati in 1874. In 1876 she learned more about pottery and glazing at an exposition in Philadelphia, which inspired her to found Rookwood Pottery in 1880.

Oldest Performing Arts Organization

Cincinnati May Festival

Cincinnati Music Hall, 1241 Elm St., Over-the-Rhine
mayfestival.com

Cincinnati May Festival is the city's oldest arts organization as well as the oldest choral festival in North America. Its roots predate the festival, which formally was launched in 1873 with eight concerts in five days. As early as 1849, German immigrants organized singing festivals or *saengerfests*, bringing performers from far and wide to be featured in choral works with local singing societies whose members were mostly men.

In 1871, **Maria Longworth Nichols** and her husband experienced a choral music festival in Europe, and that planted a seed. She invited renowned conductor Theodore Thomas (1835–1905) to discuss "a plan for a large Musical Festival" that he would conduct. The couple pledged to raise $50,000 and assembled a team of visionary community leaders to make it possible. The chorus they created for the inaugural event in 1873 had 706 singers, men and women who performed music by Handel, Bach, Beethoven, Haydn, and Mozart. The concerts were in a wood-framed venue, Saengerfest Hall, in 1873 and 1875. Starting in 1878, the festival was the initial tenant in **Cincinnati Music Hall**, the largest concert hall in America at the time, built expressly for these immense concerts. Festivals remained biennial for nearly a century; in 1967, it became an annual event with nationally and internationally acclaimed soloists and conductors.

Today, 130 volunteer singers, men and women, make up the May Festival Chorus, rehearsing year-round for springtime concerts, accompanied by the **Cincinnati Symphony Orchestra (CSO)**. Traditionally, the festival ends with a glorious rendition of the "Hallelujah Chorus" from Handel's Messiah. The chorus also performs for CSO concerts featuring choral works.

Generally, one concert is offered at Covington's historic **Cathedral Basilica of the Assumption** (1901), another venue with perfect acoustics.

Maria Longworth Nichols was just 24 years old when she spearheaded the founding of the May Festival. She also inspired philanthropist Reuben Springer to be the principal donor behind the construction of Cincinnati Music Hall, the May Festival's home.

Photo courtesy of the Cincinnati May Festival.

Oldest Concert Hall
Cincinnati Music Hall
1243 Elm St., Over-the-Rhine
cincinnatiarts.org/music-hall

Friends of Music Hall
1241 Elm St.
friendsofmusichall.org

Cincinnati Music Hall, the city's premier performance and gathering space, opened in 1878. It was built on the Elm Street site of an 1818 orphanage (later a public infirmary) and a pauper's cemetery. In the 1870s, Saengerfest Hall, a wood-frame building for German singing festivals, was built there. A noisy thunderstorm during the 1875 Cincinnati May Festival stopped the performance. Philanthropist Reuben Springer (1800–1884), who had been in the audience, was moved to offer $125,000 to construct a more permanent concert hall and convention center for industrial and agricultural expositions. His offer was contingent on raising similar funds from the community, the first-ever matching grant. With an ornate Victorian Gothic design by architect Samuel Hannaford, the monumental red brick structure cost about $300,000; the north and south exposition wings added $146,000.

The fourth May Festival on May 14, 1878, inaugurated the hall with an opera and Beethoven's Eroica Symphony. The "people's hall" had many uses. The immense main hall initially

Photo courtesy of the Cincinnati Symphony Orchestra.

could accommodate as many as 10,000 people. It hosted the 1880 Democratic National Convention. The Cincinnati Art Museum started there in the 1880s, and it was the Cincinnati Symphony Orchestra's (CSO) home from 1897 to 1912 and from 1936 onward. In 1888, the city's 100th birthday, it was the anchor for the Centennial Exposition of the Ohio Valley and Central States, which attracted more than a million visitors.

Following an extensive upgrade in 1969–1970, the Cincinnati Opera and the Cincinnati Ballet began performing there. The exposition wings became additional venues: a ballroom in the south hall and a sports arena in the north hall. Eventually, those wings provided office and backstage space for the CSO and Opera.

Between 2016 and 2018 the building was renovated dramatically ($143 million). Springer Auditorium's seating capacity was reduced from 3,600 to 2,500. The small Wilks Studio, a multi-use space, was created in the north hall. Victorian stenciling and high ceilings of Corbett Tower on the third floor were refurbished with support from the Society for the Preservation of Music Hall (now the Friends of Music Hall). Once known as Decker Hall, Corbett Tower was used through the years as a small concert venue, television studio, and destination for weddings and parties.

In 1975, Music Hall was recognized as a National Historic Landmark. Historical tours of the building's interior and exterior are offered by the Friends of Music Hall.

Since it was built on land that was once a burial ground, Music Hall has long been a destination for seekers of paranormal activity. Ghost tours are offered on a regular basis by the Friends of Music Hall.

Image courtesy of the Friends of Music Hall.

OLDEST CANAL SALOON
WASHINGTON PLATFORM SALOON & RESTAURANT
1000 Elm St., Over-the-Rhine
washingtonplatform.com

Since 1875 it's been called Washington Platform, but the building in which the restaurant and bar operates dates from the 1820s as Johan Armleder's "wine and lager beer saloon," a watering hole for people plying the **Miami and Erie Canal**. As German immigrants flooded into Cincinnati, they loved the saloon, just south of Over-the-Rhine. Armleder, an immigrant from Wurttemberg, Germany, was the owner for a half century. Its next owner, Fiedel Bader, another immigrant, renamed it Washington Platform in 1875, reminding patrons of its proximity to Washington Park, just two blocks north. In 1912, it was owned by beer baron Louis Hauck.

As with other Cincinnati bars, Washington Platform was doomed by Prohibition in 1919, the same year the decrepit canal was drained after years of disuse. The building continued as a produce store, a hand laundry, and several other businesses. Finally, in 1986, it was rechristened as Washington Platform Saloon & Restaurant and again became a destination for diners, drinkers, and out-of-town visitors. In fact, the owner expanded it in 1990 with the Canal Room, a space adjacent to the original building with many historical photos on display. Beneath Washington Platform are intact lagering cellars, a highlight of beer tours.

Photo courtesy of Rick Pender.

Oldest Pottery
Rookwood Pottery Company
1920 Race St., Over-the-Rhine
rookwood.com

Historic Rookwood Pottery Building
1077 Celestial St., Mount Adams

Maria Longworth Nichols (1849–1932) became interested in pottery–making shortly after successfully launching the first **Cincinnati May Festival** (1873). In 1880, she persuaded her father, Joseph Longworth (son of **Nicholas Longworth**), to invest in kilns and install them in a deserted schoolhouse on Eastern Avenue. She enlisted artists, a German potter, and an expert in Japanese ware. Rookwood Pottery became the first business in the United States to be owned and managed by a woman. She named the enterprise after her father's country estate in East Walnut Hills. Producing luxury earthenware and porcelain with remarkable finishes, tints, and glazes, Rookwood became recognized internationally. Following her husband's death in 1885, Maria remarried, and her interest in pottery diminished, although she remained a minority owner after 1890 until her death.

Photo courtesy of Rick Pender.

Rookwood tiles surround the entrance to the Dixie Terminal in downtown. Photo courtesy of Rick Pender.

In addition to vases, the pottery produced tiles visible in the Carew Tower Arcade and the Cincinnati Museum Center, as well as in kitchens and around fireplaces in historic homes. The Cincinnati Art Museum has a noteworthy collection of Rookwood products in its Cincinnati Wing.

The pottery was successful well into the 1920s, when it employed 200 men and women. The Depression and changes in aesthetic taste spelled its demise, and most production stopped in 1929. A series of owners failed to reestablish it until 2004, when entrepreneurs acquired the molds and located a production facility in a one-time vegetable warehouse in Over-the-Rhine near Findlay Market. With new kilns, equipment, and artistic staff, Rookwood Pottery is flourishing again, and studio tours are available.

The Rookwood Pottery building in Mount Adams, a half-timbered structure overlooking downtown Cincinnati, was erected in 1892 and expanded in 1899 and 1903. Since the 1970s, it has housed several restaurants.

Photo courtesy of Rick Pender.

Oldest Symphony Orchestra

Cincinnati Symphony Orchestra

Cincinnati Music Hall, 1241 Elm St., Over-the-Rhine
cincinnatisymphony.org, cincinnatisymphony.org/pops

The Cincinnati Symphony Orchestra (CSO) is America's fifth-oldest orchestra. It was organized by Helen Herron "Nellie" Taft (1861–1930), also known as Mrs. William Howard Taft, and gave its first concerts in 1895 at Pike's Opera House. In 1896, it settled into **Cincinnati Music Hall**, its longtime home in addition to a 24-year stint (1912–1936) at Over-the-Rhine's Emery Theatre. Frank Van der Stucken (1858–1929) was its first conductor. Among its 13 music directors have been Leopold Stokowski (1882–1977), Eugène Ysaÿe (1858-1931), Fritz Reiner (1888–1963), Eugene Goosens (1893–1962), Max Rudolf (1902–1995), Thomas Schippers (1930–1977), Jesús Lopez-Cóbos (1940–2018), Paavo Järvi (1962), and Louis Langrée (1961).

The orchestra has been responsible for several musical firsts: It performed the US premiere of Gustav Mahler's Fifth Symphony (1905) and his Third Symphony (1914). In 1966, it was the first US orchestra to undertake a world tour. It performed the world premieres of Aaron Copland's Lincoln Portrait (1942) and "Fanfare for the Common Man" (1943), a work it commissioned.

Photo courtesy of the Cincinnati Symphony Orchestra.

In addition to Music Hall, the CSO performs a summer season at Riverbend Music Center, an outdoor amphitheater east of downtown that can accommodate 20,500 attendees. The CSO has accompanied productions by the **Cincinnati Opera** since its 1920 inception, one of the longest partnerships between a symphony and an opera company in the united States. It also provides orchestral accompaniment for the Cincinnati Ballet.

The orchestra, with 91 full-time musicians, also performs as the Cincinnati Pops. In that configuration, it was founded in 1977 and led for three decades by Erich Kunzel (1935–2009); John Morris Russell (1960) is its current conductor. Under Kunzel, an energetic public figure, the Pops issued nearly 90 releases featuring classical, Broadway, and cinematic compositions. "JMR," as he's commonly known, has overseen several live recordings of iconic American folk and roots music.

OLDEST VETERANS HALL
CINCINNATI MEMORIAL HALL
1225 Elm St., Over-the-Rhine
memorialhallotr.com

Cincinnati's oldest veterans building was constructed by the Grand Army of the Republic and Hamilton County in 1908. The Hamilton County Memorial Building, part of a statewide Ohio movement to establish veterans' memorials in every county, honored soldiers, sailors, and marines with a particular focus on the Civil War and the Spanish-American War. Relics from these conflicts were placed there, including a plaque made from the metal of the USS *Maine*, blown up in Cuba's Havana harbor in 1898.

The Beaux Arts-style building was designed by **Hannaford & Sons**. Statues above the doors sculpted by Clement Barnhart (1857–1935) represent men in military uniforms from America's first century. The building's second-floor auditorium, seating 556, has words representing virtues honored by the Grand Army of the Republic painted above the proscenium: "Patriotism," "Will," "Integrity," "Manliness," "Martyrdom," and "Philanthropy." The hall features crystal chandeliers, marble staircases and hallways, and two large meeting rooms on the first floor.

Memorial Hall was used by veterans organizations for several decades; it was listed on the National Register of Historic Places in 1978. Later in the 20th century, it fell into deteriorating

Photo courtesy of Barberstock.

disuse. In 1988, the Hamilton County Board of Commissioners partnered with the Cincinnati Preservation Association for some restoration. This spurred interest in the Over-the-Rhine neighborhood, including repaving two blocks of Elm Street with granite cobblestones.

A 2016 restoration and expansion of the building by the Cincinnati Center City Development Corporation (3CDC) added air conditioning, larger restrooms, more comfortable seating, and a catering kitchen. The small stage, originally designed for lectures, was expanded to accommodate larger performances with contemporary audiovisual equipment. Memorial Hall OTR is a rejuvenated venue for special events, concerts, readings, and private gatherings such as weddings.

Oldest Parade
Reds Opening Day Findlay Market Parade
FindlayMarketParade.com

Findlay Market
1801 Race St., Over-the-Rhine
findlaymarket.org

Since the **Cincinnati Reds** was baseball's first professional team in 1869 and joined the National League in 1876, for many years it had the privilege of opening every season at home. Many seasons during the 20th century featured the Reds in an opening game a day ahead of other teams. That made Reds Opening Day a special, local holiday. That honor no longer is offered, but the team's primacy laid the foundation for a celebrated annual event: the **Findlay Market Parade**, which began in 1919 and is Cincinnati's oldest annual parade, marching pregame from the market in Over-the-Rhine to the ballpark.

It's a grassroots event, with kids skipping school and grown-ups calling the office with a 24-hour excuse so they can line downtown sidewalks to cheer the team on at the start of a new season. It's grown annually from a modest lineup of cars, trucks, and beer wagons (sometimes featuring Budweiser's Clydesdale horses), high school marching bands, and lots of politicians, to an annual rite of spring celebrated by thousands of local fans. Marking its centennial year in 2019, the parade had more than 100 units.

The Findlay Market Association sponsors the annual rite of spring, naming a grand marshal—a local personality, a celebrity baseball fan, and sometimes a past star player—to lead the parade and deliver a ball to the stadium for the first pitch.

Among the Reds longtime supporters are the "Rosie Reds," a women's organization formed in 1964. "ROSIE" stands for "Rooters Organized to Stimulate Interest and Enthusiasm." The organization donates funds raised to local colleges and universities.

Photo courtesy of the Cincinnati Enquirer.

Mount Adams
and
Eden Park

OLDEST UTILITY
CINCINNATI WATER WORKS
Throughout Eden Park

I t might seem strange to cite a public utility as historic, but Cincinnati's proximity to the Ohio River made water a key local resource. Its ready availability has made it a civic concern for more than two centuries. In March 1817, a committee was formed to oversee the building of water works. Albert Stein (1785–1874), a German immigrant, was hired to design a system to pump water from the river through iron pipes to an elevated wooden reservoir, using pumps driven by horses or oxen. It began to operate in 1820. Stein subsequently designed water works for Nashville, New York City, and New Orleans. Cincinnati Water Works became a municipally owned and operated utility in 1839.

Historic postcard.

As the city grew, so did the demand for running water. Eden Park, 200 acres of land that once featured a vineyard owned by **Nicholas Longworth**, was sold to the city in 1866. High elevation made it a suitable location for a reservoir, completed by 1878. Remnants of the water system, especially structures designed by **Samuel Hannaford**, still are present: a water tower (1894) in the form of a castle keep and an ornate pumping station (1889) crowned with gargoyles and a 172-foot standpipe. **Elsinore Castle** (1883) on Gilbert Avenue is a Hannaford-designed valve house element of this system.

The open reservoir was redeveloped as Mirror Lake, a reflecting pool, in the early 1960s. Next to it is the Spring House Gazebo (1904), an image of which is part of Cincinnati Parks's logo. The picturesque structure was the site of a shocking 1927 murder: notorious Prohibition bootlegger George Remus (1878–1952) shot and killed his wife there as she was on her way to court for a divorce hearing. His temporary insanity plea during a sensational trial kept him from jail.

Early millionaire Nicholas Longworth (1783–1863) was a land speculator interested in horticulture. He cultivated American Catawba grapes, establishing him as the "Father of American Winemaking." But a blight killed the grapevines in his Garden of Eden, and he eventually sold the land to the city, creating Eden Park.

Oldest Telescope and Observatory

Cincinnati Observatory

3489 Observatory Pl., Mount Lookout
cincinnatiobservatory.org

The Cincinnati Observatory can claim to be the oldest in several ways. Known as "the birthplace of American astronomy," it was the first public observatory in the western hemisphere. It houses one of the oldest working telescopes in the world.

It was situated initially on a hilltop east of downtown Cincinnati called Mount Ida, on land donated by **Nicholas Longworth**. When former president John Quincy Adams (1767–1848) came for its dedication on November 9, 1843, the neighborhood was renamed Mount Adams in his honor. It was the sixth president's final public speaking engagement.

Cleveland Abbe (1838–1916) was named the observatory's astronomer (1868–1870). In 1869, he began a system to assemble telegraphic weather reports and daily weather maps that made weather forecasting possible. In 1870, Congress established the US Weather Bureau in Washington, D.C., and Abbe became its first chief meteorologist.

The University of Cincinnati took over management of the observatory in 1871. In 1873, the observatory escaped downtown Cincinnati's smoky pollution when it relocated to a serene, parklike setting in Mount Lookout. Its new home in a Greek Revival building was designed by architect **Samuel Hannaford**. The East Side Cincinnati neighborhood was named "Mount Lookout" in recognition of the observatory.

The observatory has two historic telescopes: an 11-inch Merz and Mahler refractor from Munich (1845) and a 16-inch Alvan Clark & Sons refractor from Massachusetts (1904). The Observatory was designated as a National Historic Landmark in 1998.

In 1979, the observatory became part of UC's physics department. In 1999, it evolved into a nonprofit organization serving as a center for astronomy education, offering tours, viewings, and informative programs. Generations of Cincinnatians have peered through the telescopes and experienced the wonders of the universe.

The Merz and Mahler 11-inch refractor telescope, the biggest telescope in the United States in 1845, is probably the oldest continually used instrument in the world. Visitors for public education programs are still permitted to view the heavens through it.

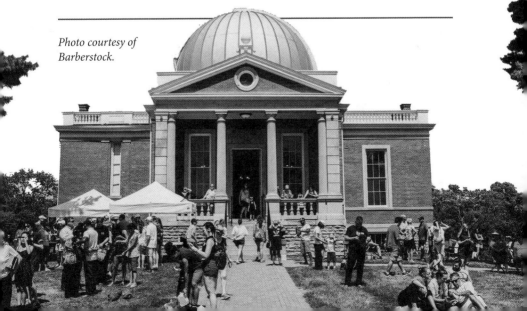

Photo courtesy of Barberstock.

Oldest Religious Observance

Holy Cross-Immaculata Church

30 Guido St., Mount Adams
hcparish.org

Holy Cross Immaculata Heart of Mary Church sits on a prominent hilltop above Mount Adams. Its cornerstone was laid by Archbishop John B. Purcell in 1859, and the

Photo courtesy of the Cincinnati Enquirer.

parish church opened late in 1860. It fulfilled a promise the archbishop made during a storm at sea: if he survived, he would build a church at the highest point in Cincinnati. While the church was under construction, at Purcell's urging, faithful parishioners took up the practice of praying on the muddy, rock-strewn hillside for the success of his venture, a shrine to the Holy Virgin. This sign of faith motivated the 1859 construction of seven flights of wooden steps from St. Gregory Street up to the church's entrance. While the daily practice eventually went by the wayside, it became a tradition for thousands of the faithful to "pray the steps" on Good Friday, two days before Easter Sunday.

In 1909, the city replaced the wooden steps with concrete ones; there were further improvements in 1958 and 2009. Nevertheless, praying the Rosary on the "Good Friday steps" remains a long-standing religious observance. Once people reach the top, it's customary to kiss the crucifix by the church's entrance. From that point, if it's a clear day, there is an exhilarating 10-mile view over the Ohio River Valley. The church was listed on the National Register of Historic Places in 1978.

The German immigrants who came by the thousands to Cincinnati in the 19th century were mostly Roman Catholics from Bavaria, especially Munich. Even today, many Cincinnati residents identify where they live by their parish rather than a neighborhood.

OLDEST ART MUSEUM
CINCINNATI ART MUSEUM
953 Eden Park Dr., Mount Adams
cincinnatiartmuseum.org

The Cincinnati Art Museum is the oldest art museum west of the Allegheny Mountains and the city's oldest year-round cultural institution. A women's museum association was established in 1877; initially, it mounted exhibitions at **Cincinnati Music Hall**. In 1881, plans were finalized to build a permanent museum in Eden Park. Heralded as "the Art Palace of the West," it opened in 1886. The original building, designed by architect James McLaughlin (1834–1925), expanded several times, with new wings added in 1907, the 1930s and '40s, and 1965.

In 2003, the museum launched the 18,000-square-foot Cincinnati Wing, the first permanent display of a city's art history in the United States. Its 15 galleries feature art created by local artists since 1788. Works by painters Frank Duveneck and Robert Scott Duncanson, **Rookwood Pottery**, art-carved furniture, and sculpture are showcased.

In 2020 the museum opened the Art Climb, a 166-step

Photo courtesy of the Cincinnati Art Museum.

installation from Gilbert Avenue to the front of the museum. It functions as an attractive approach and gateway, with stops provided along the 450-foot elevation for performances and outdoor artworks.

The museum's permanent collection encompasses more than 67,000 works, spanning 6,000 years of human history. General admission is free; frequent special exhibitions have nominal entrance fees. The Rosenthal Education Center is an immersive, family-oriented area. The Terrace Café offers indoor dining as well as seating adjacent to a lovely courtyard.

OLDEST CASTLES

ELSINORE CASTLE (ELSINORE ARCH)

1700 Gilbert Ave.

CHÂTEAU LAROCHE (LOVELAND CASTLE)

12025 Shore Dr., Loveland
lovelandcastle.com

Since Cincinnati is not a medieval city, it's a surprise to find not one but two castles here. Elsinore Arch, more commonly referred to as Elsinore Castle, was constructed on Gilbert Avenue in 1883 to house a **Cincinnati Water Works** valve. It regulated the water flow from the Eden Park reservoir into downtown Cincinnati. The structure also provided a striking entrance to Eden Park and access to a set of steep steps up the hillside to the new **Cincinnati Art Museum**.

A Shakespearean Dramatic Festival at Music Hall in May 1883 featured a production of Hamlet. Its backdrop was a large painting of Elsinore Castle, the setting for the moody tragedy. Water Works Superintendent A.G. Moore was impressed with the image and asked his brother-in-law, architect **Samuel Hannaford**, to design a valve house resembling it. In Romanesque Revival style, Hannaford created a short,

Elsinore Arch.
Photo courtesy of Rick Pender.

square, Norman tower and arch, topped with battlements. It was added to the National Register of Historic Places in 1980.

Château Laroche, sometimes called Loveland Castle, can be found 25 miles northeast of downtown. Harry D. Andrews (1890–1981), a World War I veteran and a lover of the Middle Ages, began singlehandedly to assemble it on the banks

Château Laroche.
Photo courtesy of Rick Pender.

of the Little Miami River in the 1920s, often using stones from the riverbed as well as poured concrete blocks. A Boy Scout leader, Andrews made this his singular 50-year project, assisted by generations of scouts. He willed the castle to the Knights of the Golden Trail, his Boy Scout troop. It continues to be maintained with historic artifacts from Europe as well as beautiful gardens; a self-guided tour includes a video about the castle's construction.

Samuel Hannaford and his sons, also architects, designed the fanciful water works structures found throughout Eden Park. Harvey and Charles continued their father's much admired reputation into the 20th century.

OLDEST URBAN GREENHOUSE
KROHN CONSERVATORY

1501 Eden Park Dr.
cincinnatiparks.com/krohn

Krohn Conservatory, Cincinnati's oldest greenhouse, is more than that. It is truly a botanical conservatory, dedicated to cultivating and displaying more than 3,500 plant species from around the world. It opened in 1933, replacing smaller greenhouses in Eden Park dating back to the 1880s. Using Art Deco styling, architects William Rapp (1879–1974) and his son-in-law, Standish Meacham (1889–1949), designed the building with a central entrance lobby in the form of a Gothic arch; it had an area of 22,000 square feet under glass. In 1937, the Eden Park Greenhouse,

Photo courtesy of Cincinnati Parks.

as it was originally called, was renamed to honor Irwin M. Krohn (1869–1948), who was a commissioner of the Cincinnati Park Board from 1912 to 1948.

Krohn Conservatory's principal collections include tropical plants, palms, orchids, bonsai trees, desert succulents, and cacti, as well as floral displays that are showcased in a half-dozen

Photo courtesy of the Cincinnati Park Board.

seasonal shows. Especially popular is the annual late spring Butterfly Show with live creatures flying free in a wing of the building. A holiday Poinsettia Express display, with model trains and replicas of Cincinnati buildings made of plant-based materials, is set among displays of holiday flowers.

Cincinnati's parks system includes five regional and 70 neighborhood parks as well as 34 nature preserves. It is one of the oldest and most extensive city park systems in the United States.

Oldest Professional Theater

Cincinnati Playhouse in the Park

962 Mount Adams Circle, Eden Park
cincyplay.com

The Cincinnati Playhouse in the Park is the city's oldest professional theater, one of the first regional theaters in the United States. Gerald Covell, an Oberlin College student, recruited leadership and financial support to start producing shows with Meyer Levin's *Compulsion*, which opened on October 10, 1960. The original venue was a converted 1871 Eden Park shelter house. That structure still exists within the Playhouse complex as today's 172-seat Rosenthal Shelterhouse Theatre (formerly the Jay Thompson Shelterhouse). In 1968, the Robert S. Marx Theatre, a 626-seat mainstage, was added. Plans are underway for a new 539-seat mainstage complex replacing the Marx, to open in 2022.

Original park shelterhouse. Photo courtesy of the Cincinnati Playhouse in the Park.

From 1972 to 1974, Harold Scott (1935–2006) served as the Playhouse's artistic director, the first African American to take on that responsibility at an American regional theater.

Since 1966, the Playhouse has championed new works for the stage in the US and beyond, particularly under the two-decade-long artistic leadership of Ed Stern (1946–2019). Russell Lees's *Nixon's Nixon* (1999) was produced on four continents. In 2004, the Playhouse was honored with the Regional Theatre Tony Award.

The Playhouse's 2007 revival staging of Stephen Sondheim and George Furth's musical *Company*, directed by Tony Award winner John Doyle, was moved to Broadway and recognized the 2007 Tony Award for Best Revival of a Musical. The Playhouse is one of very few theaters in the United States to have won two Tonys.

Using its two theaters, the Playhouse in the Park produces 10 shows annually, including a beloved staging of an adaptation of Charles Dickens's A Christmas Carol, a local holiday tradition for more than three decades.

NORTH

OLDEST STAGECOACH INN
GOLDEN LAMB INN & RESTAURANT

27 S Broadway, Lebanon, OH 45036
goldenlamb.com

The Golden Lamb Inn was licensed on December 23, 1803, as a "house of Public Entertainment" on Broadway in Lebanon, Ohio. Jonas Seaman, whose father was a tavern keeper in New Jersey, bought the license for $4 and built a two-story log building in the center of the newly established village. He hung out a sign with the image of a golden lamb, since many early travelers could not read. His wife, Martha, was a cook, and the entire family created a tavern that became known as a preferred stop for meals or to spend the night while traveling to or from Cincinnati along the National Road, today's US Route 40. Over time it's accommodated many travelers, including a dozen US presidents, from Ohio's own William Henry Harrison in 1825 and John Quincy Adams in 1843 on his way to Cincinnati for the dedication of the **Cincinnati Observatory** to Ronald Reagan in 1968 and George W. Bush in 2005. Other luminaries, such as sharpshooter Annie Oakley, astronaut Neil Armstrong, and writers Charles Dickens, Harriet Beecher Stowe, and Mark Twain, have visited, too.

The inn's restaurant is a year-round dining destination for formal dining or more casual fare in the adjacent Black Horse Tavern. Since 2018, it has operated its own farm, raising vegetables, herbs, and melons for daily fare. There's also a field of popcorn, a berry patch, and several beehives.

The Golden Lamb is, in fact, the oldest hotel in Ohio. In the 21st century, it's become a popular stop for political candidates, perhaps wishing to tie their campaigns to the many presidents who spent the night there.

Photo courtesy of The Golden Lamb.

OLDEST UNIVERSITY
UNIVERSITY OF CINCINNATI

2600 Clifton Ave.
uc.edu

Cincinnati's oldest institution of higher education is the University of Cincinnati (UC), which dates its establishment to 1819. In that year, Dr. Daniel Drake (1785–1852) founded Cincinnati College and the Medical College of Ohio. Its early home was in downtown Cincinnati. It closed in 1825 due to financial difficulties; Drake, a renowned physician and scientist, reestablished it in 1835, when it combined forces with the Cincinnati Law School.

In 1858, the estate of Charles McMicken (1782–1858) was allocated to the city of Cincinnati to establish a university;

McMicken Hall.
Photo courtesy of Rick Pender.

bringing together the institutions Drake founded, UC constructed its first buildings on Clifton Avenue and was chartered by the Ohio legislature. Its colleges eventually included law, medicine, education, arts and sciences, pharmacy, art, architecture and design, business, music, and performing arts.

The university was designated as a "municipally-sponsored, state-affiliated" institution in 1968; in 1977, it became a state institution officially. Noteworthy achievements of UC researchers include the 1941 creation of the antihistamine Benadryl® by George Rieveschl (1916–2007) and the development of the oral polio vaccine in 1960 by Albert Sabin (1906–1993). Astronaut Neil Armstrong (1930–2012), the first man to walk on the moon, taught aerospace engineering at UC from 1971 to 1979. Notable alumni include basketball star Oscar Robinson (b. 1938), all-star baseball pitcher Sandy Koufax (b. 1935), and architect Michael Graves (b. 1934).

Today's UC enrolls 44,000 students, the second-largest university in Ohio. Its main campus is located in Clifton Heights; there are branch campuses in the northeastern suburb of Blue Ash and Batavia, in Clermont County. The university also owns the historic **Cincinnati Observatory** in Mount Lookout.

Medical pioneer Dr. Daniel Drake also founded Cincinnati's Commercial Hospital and Lunatic Asylum, which became Cincinnati Hospital then General Hospital, and finally today's University Hospital.

Oldest Presidential Sites

William Howard Taft National Historic Site
2038 Auburn Ave.,
Mount Auburn
nps.gov/wiho/index.htm

Taft's Ale House
1429 Race St., Over-the-Rhine
taftsalehouse.com

Harrison Tomb State Memorial
41 Cliff Rd., North Bend, OH
hmsfmuseum.org

Grant Birthplace
1551 State Rte. 232,
Point Pleasant, OH
usgrantbirthplace.org

America's 27th president, William Howard Taft (1857–1930), was born in Cincinnati. His childhood home and birthplace in Mount Auburn is a National Historic Site. The house where Taft spent his childhood was purchased by his father, Alphonso, in 1851. It has been restored authentically, including family portraits and books. The second floor contains exhibits of Taft's accomplishments.

Educated at Yale University, Taft attended law school at the University of Cincinnati, held several governmental positions and eventually became dean of the law school. He was ambassador to the Philippines (1901–1903) and Secretary of War under Theodore Roosevelt (1904–1908). Taft served as US president

Harrison Tomb Site Memorial.
Photo courtesy of Rick Pender.

William H. Taft Birthplace.
Photo courtesy of Getty Images.

himself (1909–1913) and was appointed the tenth chief justice of the US Supreme Court in 1920, a position he held until just before his death in 1930, making him the only person to serve as president and a member of the Supreme Court.

Décor details from the Taft birthplace including floor tiles, wallpaper, and furnishings, as well as historic photos of Taft and his wife, Nellie, can be seen in Taft's Ale House, a popular Over-the-Rhine craft brewery renovated in 2015 from the abandoned St. Paul's German Evangelical Church (1850).

America's ninth president, William Henry Harrison (1773–1841), was born in Virginia but spent most of his adult life in southwest Ohio on a farm in North Bend, 15 miles west of Cincinnati. He died of pneumonia after just one month in office in 1841. His tomb is a state memorial, a 60-foot monument at the summit of Mount Nebo in North Bend, overlooking the Ohio River. Civil War general and the nation's 18th president, Ulysses S. Grant (1822–1885), was born and lived in modest homes in Point Pleasant and Georgetown, Ohio, 57 miles east of Cincinnati.

When William H. Taft accepted his nomination for the presidency in 1908, he did so from the front portico of another Cincinnati landmark: The historic 1820 home of his half-brother Charles Phelps Taft, today's Taft Museum of Art.

OLDEST CEMETERIES

SPRING GROVE CEMETERY
4521 Spring Grove Ave.
springgrove.org

OLD JEWISH CEMETERY (CHESTNUT STREET CEMETERY)
Chestnut St. at Central Ave.
jcemcin.org

UNITED AMERICAN CEMETERY
Duck Creek Rd., Madisonville
unionbaptist.net

UNION BAPTIST CEMETERY
4933 Cleves-Warsaw Rd.,
Price Hill
unionbaptist.net

The Pioneer Cemetery in **Columbia-Tusculum** (1790) is the area's oldest. But Cincinnati has several historic cemeteries, especially Spring Grove Cemetery and Arboretum (1845), the second-largest in the United States. In 1844, members of the Cincinnati Horticultural Society, inspired by rural cemeteries in Paris and elsewhere, formed a cemetery association. Attorney Salmon P. Chase (1808–1873), eventually Ohio's governor and chief justice of the US Supreme Court, and others drew up articles of incorporation. On September 1, 1845, the first burial took place. Named for its numerous springs and groves on the 733-acre property, Spring Grove was more than a cemetery. In 1855, renowned landscape architect Adolph Strauch (1822–1883) was hired to beautify the grounds; his plan, using lakes, trees, and shrubs, remains profoundly evident. It has 44 miles of winding roads, 15 lakes, and 1,200 plant species. Numerous eminent Cincinnatians were buried there: abolitionist Levi Coffin (1798–1877), grocer Barney Kroger (1860-1938), architect **Samuel**

Hannaford, and millionaire **Nicholas Longworth**, as well as 41 Civil War generals. Hannaford designed Norman Chapel (1880) near the main entrance gate, a Romanesque Revival structure with stained glass windows. Spring Grove is a National Historic Landmark (2007); the chapel is on the National Register of Historic Places (1980).

The Old Jewish Cemetery was established in 1821 in Cincinnati's Betts-Longworth Historic District, today a tiny plot enclosed by high walls and a locked gate. In 1821, Benjamin Lieb, a member of the city's tiny first Jewish congregation, hoped for a Jewish cemetery where he could be buried. The congregation, K. K. Bene Israel, had no cemetery or synagogue, so a plot of land was purchased from Nicholas Longworth for $75. It is the oldest Jewish cemetery west of the Allegheny Mountains. First called the Chestnut Street Cemetery, it was filled to capacity by a cholera epidemic in 1849 and closed with 85 graves.

The United American Cemetery on Duck Creek near Strathmore Drive is Ohio's oldest cemetery for Black people. Burials began in 1832 in Avondale, but in 1883 racist sentiment forced the removal of graves to a segregated site on 11.5 acres in Madisonville. It's operated by the Union Baptist Church, organized in 1831 when Black members of a predominantly white congregation formed their own church. The church also manages the Union Baptist Cemetery (1864), another historic burial ground still used by a Black congregation. Many former slaves, anti-slavery advocates, and supporters of the Underground Railroad were interred there.

Norman Chapel at Spring Grove Cemetery. Photo courtesy of Rick Pender.

OLDEST HOSPITALS
MERCY HEALTH JEWISH HOSPITAL
4777 E Galbraith Rd., Kenwood
mercy.com

GOOD SAMARITAN HOSPITAL
375 Dixmyth Ave., Clifton Heights
trihealth.com

As Cincinnati grew in the 19th century, the need for health care led several religious institutions to establish hospitals. The first Jewish hospital in the United States came about following a cholera epidemic in 1849. Opening in 1850 in a house on Central Avenue near the Jewish community in the city's West End, it was non-sectarian and philanthropic. In 1882, it opened a retirement home in Avondale, and in 1890 built a new hospital there. A nursing home was added in 1892. In 1987, a 664-bed hospital with 19 departments opened at 3200 Burnet Ave. In 1988, Otto C. Epp Memorial Hospital (1960) was acquired in suburban Kenwood. In 1997, the Burnet Avenue hospital closed, and services moved to Kenwood. In 2010 the Jewish Foundation

Jewish Hospital, Cincinnati, Ohio.

Photo courtesy of cincinativiews.net.

THE GOOD SAMARITAN HOSPITAL, CINCINNATI, OHIO.

Mariemont Players' Walton Creek Theatre. Photo courtesy of cincinativiews.net.

sold the Kenwood hospital to Mercy Health, which invested in technology and infrastructure. The hospital maintains close ties to the Jewish community.

In 1852, Roman Catholic Archbishop John Purcell identified a need for a hospital to care for needy people. A one-time school in Over-the-Rhine was converted to a 21-bed facility run by the Sisters of Charity of Cincinnati. Within three years, Cincinnati's first private hospital cared for more than 1,500 patients and needed a larger facility. It relocated to an old mansion at Third and Plum streets. Called St. John's Hospital, it provided care for men and women injured during the Civil War. In 1866, operations moved to a 95-bed facility on Sixth Street, the Hospital of the Good Samaritan, where care was offered to anyone, regardless of race or religion. A school of nursing began in 1897.

By 1907, a five-bed annex was located at Clifton and Resor avenues. During the next decade, more nearby land was secured. Over several years, the sisters bought more land and moved the entire hospital to a two-wing facility on Clifton Avenue. It was expanded in 1927, 1959, and 1985. "Good Sam" has delivered more babies than any other hospital in Ohio.

Oldest Planned Communities

Glendale Heritage Preservation Museum
44 Village Sq., Glendale, OH
glendaleheritage.org

Glendale Lyceum
865 Congress Ave.,
Glendale, OH
GlendaleLyceum.com

Mary M. Emery Memorial Carillon in Dogwood Park
3721 Pleasant St., Mariemont, OH

Glendale, 15 miles north of downtown Cincinnati, was America's first planned suburban community. The railroad commuter town sits along a still-active train track that enabled easy travel for wealthy businessmen to the urban core. The picturesque suburban community was envisioned in 1851 by the Glendale Association, a group of civic leaders, many associated with Procter & Gamble or the railroad. Streets were laid out in a pattern following the rolling topography, and the town included four landscaped parks and a small lake, very much in the style developed for rural cemeteries, including Cincinnati's **Spring Grove Cemetery**. The first large home in Glendale was built in 1854 for banker H.W. Hughes. Homes in the nearly 400-acre historic district mostly are Italianate or Second Empire architecture, prevalent in the 1850s. The village's 1880 Cincinnati, Hamilton, and Dayton railroad depot today is a museum of memorabilia. The district was designated a National Historic Landmark in 1977.

The Glendale Lyceum is a private, member-run social club, incorporated in 1883. Its elegant clubhouse was built in 1891. The club's goal is to promote higher education and social and friendly relations among members, and to provide literary, musical, and social entertainment for members, the Village of Glendale, and surrounding neighborhoods.

Mariemont, 10 miles east of downtown Cincinnati, was another planned community, developed in the 1920s by philanthropist Mary Emery (1844–1927) and landscape architect John Nolen. Emery sought to alleviate housing shortages and poor housing conditions after World War I. Nolen's plan, accepted in 1921, took about a decade to develop. Mariemont resembles an English country village, featuring much Tudor Revival architecture and a stone English country church. There are several large parks, including Dogwood Park with its Emery Memorial Carillon. The village was designated a National Historic Landmark in 2007.

Photo courtesy of glendalelyceum.com.

OLDEST GERMAN RESTAURANT
MECKLENBURG GARDENS

302 E University Ave., Corryville
mecklenburgs.com

Cincinnati is a distinctly German city, and one-time headwaiter Louis Mecklenburg recognized that in 1886 when he became the owner of the Mount Auburn Garden Restaurant. It started in 1870 in a building constructed as a home in 1865. Mecklenburg Restaurant and Bier Garten changed from a saloon to a German beer garden, catering to the massive influx of immigrants. Today, Mecklenburg Gardens is Cincinnati's oldest German restaurant, offering both authentic atmosphere and cuisine. Particularly popular is its outdoor beer garden, roofed with century-old, leafy grapevines.

It has a storied existence. It stayed in business as a speakeasy during Prohibition, selling illegal liquor to patrons who knew the all-clear signal: the position of a model ship on the bar. In the 1970s, it underwent a structural restoration that landed the building on the National Register of Historic Places (1976). It was owned by an ashram involved in Eastern spiritualism and meditation that was accused eventually of brainwashing one of the chefs. Influenced or not, his kitchen won four Mobil Travel Guide stars for the restaurant. Today, it's a gathering place for German heritage groups where traditional lagers and pilsners can be quaffed, and German fare dominates the menu.

Photo courtesy of Mecklenburg Gardens.

Oldest Zoo
Cincinnati Zoo & Botanical Garden
3400 Vine St., Avondale
cincinnatizoo.org

There's just one zoo in Cincinnati, so naturally it's the oldest. But the Cincinnati Zoo & Botanical Garden truly has been around a long time since opening in 1875. In fact, it's the second-oldest public zoo in the United States. The Reptile House, built as the Monkey House in 1875, is the oldest zoo building in the country. The Zoo's original collection was modest: eight monkeys, two grizzly bears, three deer, six raccoons, two elk, a buffalo, a hyena, a tiger, an alligator, a circus elephant, and more than 400 birds. It's grown considerably: today there are nearly 2,000 animals, representing more than 500 species as well as 3,000 distinct plant species.

The Zoo's founder, Andrew Erkenbrecher (1821–1885), a successful merchant who produced and sold laundry starch from a factory in St. Bernard, began his impact on the natural world as the president of the "Society for the Acclimatization of Birds." In 1872 the society brought 1,000 insect-eating birds to Cincinnati from Europe to control an infestation of caterpillars. Erkenbrecher and his colleagues began discussing the creation of a zoo and acquired 65 acres of land in a cow pasture, today's Avondale neighborhood. Over the years, the Zoo has become as renowned for its lush floral gardens and landscaping as for its animal habitats. It became a National Historic Landmark in

Photo courtesy of the Cincinnati Enquirer *Archives.*

1987. Readers of *USA Today* named it North America's top zoo in 2019.

The Zoo was the home of Martha, the last passenger pigeon, who died in 1914. Over the years, the Zoo has conducted numerous successful breeding programs. In 1986, it created the Center for Conservation and Research of Endangered Wildlife (CREW) to help save endangered species, such as lowland gorillas. In 2017, Fiona, a prematurely born hippopotamus, was nursed toward healthy adulthood and media stardom.

The Zoo has several unusual exhibits including the "World of the Insect" and "Night Hunters," a multi-sensory journey through the wild at night. A popular annual event is "Zoo Babies," a springtime show of irresistible new offspring.

Oldest Jewish Institution

Hebrew Union College

3101 Clifton Ave., Clifton Hts.
huc.edu

Cincinnati Skirball Museum

Founded in 1875, Hebrew Union College is Cincinnati's oldest Jewish institution. It was founded by Rabbi Isaac M. Wise, the American Reform Judaism leader who established Bene Yeshurum in 1854, the sect's first congregation. Reform Judaism was less ruled by orthodox dietary laws and practiced with fewer rituals and mandatory prayers. Services were conducted in English, and no longer were men and women segregated in the **Isaac M. Wise Temple** (1866). Until Wise's death in 1900, he was the editor of the still-published *American Israelite*, the oldest Jewish newspaper in the United States.

As Wise began to spread his ideas and influence across the United States, it was a challenge to find rabbis who could serve in the new temples. Accordingly, he established the Union of American Hebrew Congregations (1873). In 1875, 72 congregations came together to found Hebrew Union College on Clifton Avenue, not far from the University of Cincinnati, with which it exchanged some students and professors. Wise served as president of the seminary for training rabbis, cantors, educators, and workers. Sallie Priesand, the first female rabbi in the United States, graduated from HUC in 1972.

In addition to the Cincinnati campus, Hebrew Union College-Jewish Institute of Religion has locations in New York City and Los Angeles, as well as Jerusalem, the only seminary in Israel that trains Reform Jewish clergy. Skirball Museum, located on the Cincinnati campus, is one of the oldest repositories of Jewish cultural artifacts in the United States.

Hebrew Union is the oldest extant Jewish seminary in the Americas. Its remote campus in Jerusalem is the only seminary in Israel where Reform Jewish clergy are trained.

Photo courtesy of Rick Pender.

Oldest Children's Hospital

Children's Hospital Medical Center

3333 Burnet Ave., Avondale
cincinnatichildrens.com

T hree influential, civic-minded women led by philanthropist Mary Emery (1844–1927) won support from their Episcopal bishop to open a hospital for children as a project of the diocese. In the late 19th century, hospitals generally were only for the poor or very sick as a place to die. Children and adults were placed side by side, exposed to all kinds of diseases. The Hospital of the Protestant Episcopal

Church—today's Cincinnati Children's Hospital Medical Center—opened in 1884 in a rented, three-bedroom house with 12 beds in Walnut Hills. It provided free care without regard to race or religion. A few years later, Mary Emery's husband, Thomas, and his brother, J. Josiah Emery, purchased land in Mount Auburn and built a three-story, brick, 20-bed hospital, which opened in 1887.

In 1926, the hospital moved to a new 200-bed facility near the University of Cincinnati's (UC) College of Medicine on Burnet Avenue. William Cooper Procter, one of the founders of Procter & Gamble, established the hospital's research endowment in the 1920s. Today, it is one of America's most respected pediatric hospitals, where several medical breakthroughs made history, especially the 1960 development of the oral polio vaccine by Dr. Albert Sabin (1906–1993). In the 21st century, Children's Hospital Medical Center has a sprawling campus with 634 beds, plus numerous satellite locations across southwest Ohio. With a medical staff of more than 1,500 and 16,500 total employees, it's the region's second-largest employer. Thanks to its affiliation with UC, Cincinnati Children's pediatric residency training program is one of the largest in the United States, graduating about 200 physicians annually.

Adjacent to Children's Hospital on Erkenbrecher Avenue is the largest Ronald McDonald House in the world. It has 177 rooms available without charge for families needing weeks or months of accommodation while children are being treated.

Oldest Community Theaters

CenterStage Players, Inc.
Lockland High School Auditorium, 249 W Forrer St.
centerstageplayerinc.com

Westwood Town Hall
3018 Harrison Ave., Westwood
cincinnatiparks.com

The Footlighters, Inc.
802 York St., Newport
footlighters.org

Walton Creek Theatre
4101 Walton Creek Rd., Plainville
MariemontPlayers.com

The Drama Workshop
3716 Glenmore Ave., Cheviot
thedramaworkshop.org

Cincinnati has numerous community theaters that serve specific neighborhoods. Several have historic roots or perform in historic venues. The oldest community theater in Ohio is CenterStage Players Inc., originally established as Wyoming Players in 1885. In 2005, it changed its name and moved to nearby Lockland High School.

Westwood Town Hall, built in 1889 and operated by Cincinnati Parks, is not a true theater, but it has been the venue for productions by numerous amateur companies. With a National Register designation (1974), it continues to anchor the Westwood Town Center Historic District and serve as the focal point of Cincinnati's largest neighborhood.

Mariemont Players Inc., which began as a church group in the 1930s, in 1960 acquired a two-story, four-room brick schoolhouse just east of the village and converted it into the Walton Creek Theatre. The building's schoolhouse cornerstone was laid in 1869. With several physical updates over the years, it's an excellent, if intimate, performance venue.

The Drama Workshop has been around since 1954, one of those companies that made use of the Westwood Town Hall. Now, they have their own theater in Cheviot, the Glenmore Playhouse, that was originally the Glenmore Bowl (1932), the city's oldest bowling alley.

Footlighters, Inc., which began in 1963, was another onetime Westwood Town Hall tenant. In 1988, it acquired a historic but threatened property in Newport, Kentucky, the **Salem United Methodist Church**. Designed by legendary architect **Samuel Hannaford**, it was placed on the National Register of Historic Places in 1986. Footlighters adapted it into the Stained Glass Theatre, where performances are staged in the church's onetime sanctuary.

Mariemont Players' Walton Creek Theatre. Photo courtesy of Rick Pender.

OLDEST OPERA HOUSE
SORG OPERA HOUSE
63 S Main St., Middletown, OH
sorgoperahouse.org

Sorg Opera House in Middletown was built by businessman, philanthropist, and member of the US House of Representatives (1894–1896), Paul J. Sorg (1840–1902), born in Wheeling, West Virginia, to German immigrants. His family moved to Cincinnati in 1851; when Sorg was 24, he began working in the tobacco industry, using bookkeeping skills he learned in night school. With his partner, John Auer, they moved their successful company, eventually the third-largest manufacturer of chewing tobacco in the United States, to Middletown in 1878. Sorg became a major employer and recruited other manufacturers to the city.

A multimillionaire, Sorg commissioned the opera house, designed by **Samuel Hannaford** with a pair of curved balconies and 1,200 seats. In 1901, the Sorg began to show early motion pictures and serve as a venue for operas, plays, and vaudeville performers. Entertainers over the years included Will Rogers, Al Jolson, Sophie Tucker, and Bob Hope, early in their careers. Live shows stopped in the late 1920s, when a sound system made it possible to operate as a full-time movie house. A 1935 fire did considerable damage backstage, but the theater recovered and operated as the Colonial Theater, showing movies into the 1970s.

A water main break in 2010 forced the Sorg's closure, but a group of investors acquired it in 2012 and undertook significant renovations, reopening in 2017. Remodeling reduced the seating to 737. The opera house is in Middletown's commercial district, named to the National Register of Historic Places in 2014.

The acoustics of the Sorg Opera House have been favorably compared to Carnegie Hall in New York City. It's an inviting venue for all varieties of music, from classical ensembles to rock bands.

Photo courtesy of sorgoperahouse.org.

Oldest Tennis Tournament

Western & Southern Open Cincinnati Masters

250 E Fifth St.
wsopen.com

Lindner Family Tennis Center

5460 Courseview Dr., Mason

T he oldest tennis tournament in the United States played in its original city is the Cincinnati Masters, sponsored by Western & Southern Financial Group. It first was held on September 18, 1899, at the Avondale Athletic Club. The *Cincinnati Times-Star* described the first event as being "marked with brilliant and fast playing on the part of contestants, awakening the greatest interest in what promises to be the most successful tournament ever held in Cincinnati, if not in the entire West."

In 1899 it was called the Cincinnati Open. In 1901 it became the Tri-State Tennis Tournament, a title used until 1969 for competition at the Cincinnati Tennis Club in East Walnut Hills. Paul Flory (1922–2013),

Photo courtesy of Western & Southern Open.

an executive with Procter & Gamble, became the tournament director in 1975, when the tournament was held at the **Old Coney Amusement Park** in Anderson Township. Flory oversaw the tournament's 1979 move to Mason, Ohio, in Clermont County, 25 miles northeast of downtown Cincinnati, where a permanent stadium was built. He was responsible for the tournament's growth and remained involved until his death.

Through 120 years of competition, more than 100 international Tennis Hall of Famers played in Cincinnati. The event generated millions of dollars for charities, including Cincinnati Children's Hospital Medical Center. In 2008, the tournament was sold to the United States Tennis Association, owners of the US Open.

Today the Cincinnati Masters, an annual, outdoor, hardcourt tennis event, is the second-largest summer tennis event in the United States. The Lindner Family Tennis Center in Mason has a total of 17 courts, including four tennis stadiums. The Center Court stadium can seat 11,400 fans. The tournament's present-day trophy comes from the **Rookwood Pottery Company**.

For many years only men competed in the tennis tournament, but a women's tournament was launched in 2004. As of 2011 it became a joint tournament with men's and women's competitions happening simultaneously.

Oldest Movie Theaters

Bogart's
2621 Vine St., Corryville
bogarts.com

Esquire
320 Ludlow Ave, Clifton
esquiretheatre.com

Woodward Theater
1404 Main St., Over-the-Rhine
woodwardtheater.com

Parkland Theatre
6550 Parkland Ave., Sayler Park
parklandtheatre.com

Early movie theaters where silent films were first screened charged five cents for admission, so they were called "nickelodeons." Bogart's, today's live music venue in Corryville, began as the Nordland Plaza Nickelodeon in 1905. It continued as a vaudeville theater until 1955. In the 1960s, briefly it was a German movie house and then a restaurant. It became a successful music venue in the mid-1970s.

The Esquire on Ludlow Avenue in Clifton is a mecca for independent and foreign films today. When it began in 1911, it offered silent films and live events with seating for 500. When it closed in 1983, developers proposed replacing it with a fast-food restaurant. However, local residents fought to preserve the Esquire, which reopened in 1990. With some added space, it now offers six screens, with a total seating capacity of 730.

Main Street's Woodward Theater opened in 1913 in Over-the-Rhine, showing silent movies. That ended in 1933, when it became a used car dealership. It later morphed into a Kroger's grocery store (1942–1961) and Greg's Antiques (1997–2012). As of 2015, it returned to entertainment—mostly live music,

Photo courtesy of Rick Pender.

but also community events and private parties. Coming full circle a century later, films are screened there occasionally. The Woodward's historic illuminated copper marquee was restored by its owners in 2019.

Sayler Park's Parkland Theater was built in 1881 as a vaudeville venue. It became a movie house in the 1920s. In the 1950s, it added a bar and showed R-rated films. With new owners as of 2005, it now shows family-oriented films, often with religious themes.

Woodward Theater.
Photo courtesy of Rick Pender.

Oldest Radio and TV Stations

WLW-AM (700 WLW)

8044 Montgomery Rd., Ste. 650
700wlw.iheart.com

The National Voice of America Museum of Broadcasting

8070 Tylersville Rd., West Chester
voamuseum.org

Cincinnati inventor and entrepreneur Powel Crosley Jr. (1886–1961) began manufacturing radios in 1921. To provide programming, he experimented with transmitters. On March 22, 1922, his Crosley Broadcasting Corporation

Powel Crosley Jr. at the controls.
Photo courtesy of Getty Images.

received a commercial license to operate WLW-AM at 50 watts. Power was expanded several times, and in 1932 WLW's distinctive, diamond-shaped antenna was erected in Mason, Ohio, as well as six 200,000-watt shortwave radio transmitters requested by the US government for the Voice of America. Two years later, "the Nation's station" began to broadcast from a 500,000-watt transmitter as the world's most powerful commercial radio station.

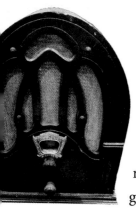

Crosley radio. Photo courtesy of the National Voice of America Museum of Broadcasting.

In 1939, the FCC ordered WLW to reduce its power because its signal was disrupting other stations. During World War II, WLW resumed periodic 500-kilowatt transmissions with government approval. Programming was heard as far away as South America and Europe. In 1962, WLW was granted approval as a "Clear Channel Broadcasting Service" at 700 khz on the AM dial.

In 1942, WLW moved to Crosley Square at 140 W 9th St. in downtown Cincinnati. In 1948, it was joined by a television station, WLW-T. Today it's WLWT-TV 5, Cincinnati's oldest TV station. Many Cincinnati TV stars—Ruth Lyons, Paul Dixon, and Bob Braun—performed their local shows there, carried on numerous stations across the Midwest.

Numerous entertainers performed from WLW's studios: jazz pianist Fats Waller; comedian Red Skelton; singers Doris Day, Rosemary Clooney, and Andy Williams; and the Mills Brothers, a popular African American vocal quartet. In 1933, WLW produced *Ma Perkins*, the first "soap opera," a serialized daily drama sponsored by

Ruth Lyons. Photo courtesy of tvhistory.com.

soap manufacturer **Procter & Gamble**. In 1937, WLW radio also produced *Midwestern Hayride*, one of the first country music shows. It continued on WLWT-TV into the 1970s.

The National Voice of America Museum of Broadcasting, including the Gray History of Wireless Museum, features exhibits about Cincinnati broadcasting.

OLDEST OPERA COMPANY
CINCINNATI OPERA

Cincinnati Music Hall, 1243 Elm St., Over-the-Rhine
cincinnatiopera.org

Cincinnati Opera began presenting productions on June 27, 1920. It's America's second-oldest opera company (only New York City's Metropolitan Opera has been at it longer). It was a hit from the get-go: Its first production, Friedrich von Flotow's 1847 German-language opera, *Martha*, sold out at the **Cincinnati Zoo** Pavilion, the summer opera's venue for a half century. The Zoo was a storied setting, with animals sometimes competing with vocalizing singers on hot summer nights. That didn't dampen anyone's enthusiasm for the art form, and Cincinnati Opera gave audiences lots of productions, sometimes as many as 18 different works receiving 61 performances during a 10-week season. Many famous singers found their way to Cincinnati to perform during those summer festivals: Norman Treigle, Beverly Sills, Montserrat Caballé, James Morris, and Roberta Peters.

Photo courtesy of Cincinnati Opera.

In 1972, Cincinnati Opera left the Zoo for historic **Cincinnati Music Hall,** renovated thanks to generous arts patrons Ralph

Photo courtesy of Cincinnati Opera.

(1897–1988) and Patricia (1908–2008) Corbett. The large hall provided a chance for bigger, more ambitious and lavish productions. The company's Wild-West staging of Donizetti's 1832 comic opera *Elixir of Love* was broadcast nationally on PBS in 1978. At both the Zoo and Music Hall, Cincinnati Opera productions have been accompanied by the Cincinnati Symphony Orchestra, one of the longest such partnerships in the arts across the United States.

As one of America's most respected opera companies, Cincinnati Opera has continued with summer productions of classics and new works—some of which it has commissioned and workshopped—that keep audiences returning to Music Hall, beautifully renovated again in 2018.

Beverly Sills performed with Cincinnati Opera.
Photo courtesy of Cincinnati Opera.

Oldest Fireworks Company

Rozzi's Famous Fireworks

118 Karl Brown Way, Loveland
rozzifireworks.com

Paolo Rozzi founded a fireworks company in 1895 in Pietramelara, Italy, near Naples. He emigrated to Pennsylvania. In 1930, Paolo's son, Arthur Rozzi Sr., and his sons, Joseph and Paul, relocated Rozzi's Famous Fireworks to Cincinnati. The fifth-generation company, now managed by Joseph's daughter, Nancy, is well-known around the world. It continues to bring award-winning, innovative displays and pyrotechnic craftsmanship to audiences around the world. The company has produced and executed more than 300 displays in cities including Cannes, France; Hannover, Germany; Surfers

Photo courtesy of cincinnatiusa.com.

Paradise, Australia; Montreal, Canada; Blackpool, England; Knokke, Belgium; and Moscow, Russia.

Rozzi's is beloved to Cincinnatians, thanks to its shows for the annual Cincinnati Riverfest on Labor Day weekend, with fireworks launched from barges in the Ohio River. The display originated in 1977 to celebrate the tenth anniversary of radio station WEBN-FM, and has continued annually ever since. Typically, the show attracts nearly 500,000 people to the shores of the Ohio River—as well as 2,500 boats on the river—to watch fireworks choreographed to a rock-and-roll musical score provided by the radio station.

After four decades, Cincinnati Riverfest has evolved into an all-day annual event on the Sunday before Labor Day. The Rubber Duck Regatta, benefiting the Freestore Foodbank, releases thousands of toy ducks into the Ohio River, for a race.

1941

OLDEST DINER
SUGAR N' SPICE DINER

4381 Reading Rd., Paddock Hills
1203 Sycamore St., Over-the-Rhine
EatSugarnSpice.com

Sugar n' Spice has been serving "wispy-thin pancakes" at its original location since Mort Keller opened the restaurant in 1941. It's offered a breakfast-and-lunch menu for the better part of eight decades: oversized omelets, sandwiches, and more have kept customers coming back regularly to the iconic, hot-pink destination. The clientele is diverse, from college students to grandparents, construction workers to doctors. Children have the opportunity to choose from a variety of

Photo courtesy of Rick Pender.

small rubber ducks to take home after dining (about 1,000 are given away weekly).

Adam Mayerson, the sixth owner of this family-owned establishment, has expanded its reach with an Over-the-Rhine location that opened in 2020 in a longtime diner on Sycamore Street. Remodeled in the colorful style of its sister location, this diner is another "oldest" candidate: Cincinnati's oldest 1950s-style diner, it's attached to a larger dining room.

OLDEST ROCK & ROLL VENUES

LUDLOW GARAGE
342 Ludlow Ave., Clifton
ludlowgaragecincinnati.com

BOGART'S
2621 Vine St., Corryville
bogarts.com

WOODWARD THEATER
1404 Main St., Over-the-Rhine
woodwardtheater.com

SOUTHGATE HOUSE REVIVAL
111 E 6th St., Newport
southgatehouse.com

The Ludlow Garage began as an automobile shop in Clifton. But it became famous as the city's first rock-and-roll venue, from September 1969 to January 1971, managed by concert promoter Jim Tarbell (b. 1942), who went on to local fame as the owner of **Arnold's Bar & Grill** and a member of the Cincinnati City Council. The Allman Brothers Band's album, *Live at Ludlow Garage: 1970*, was recorded at the club. Other well-known acts and musicians back in the day included Santana, The James Gang, Grand Funk Railroad, Taj Mahal, The Kinks, Iggy Pop and the Stooges,

Photo courtesy of Rick Pender.

B.B. King, and Alice Cooper. In 2015, new owners returned the space, which had hosted restaurants and retail over the intervening years, to a 500-seat music venue.

Since 1980, Bogart's has been the city's go-to venue for rock-and-roll. The building, opened in 1905 as the Nordland Plaza Nickelodeon, was a movie theater for more than a half century. Briefly a restaurant in the 1970s, it was remodeled as a concert venue with a 1,500-seat capacity. James Brown, Pearl Jam, The Ramones, Beastie Boys, and The Strokes all performed there.

Several other music venues have histories. One is the **Woodward Theater** in Over-the-Rhine, opened in 1913 as a movie theater. It hosted various businesses—a used car dealership, a grocery, an antique shop—before the owners of MOTR Pub bought it in 2013 and restored it as a performance venue. The other is Newport's Southgate House Revival, formerly the Grace Methodist Episcopal Church (built in 1866). Indie bands stop there to perform in The Sanctuary, The Lounge, or The Revival Room. This venue was the successor to the original Southgate House (1814 home of a Newport founder), a music venue from 1976 to 2011.

Photo courtesy of Rick Pender.

Oldest Roller Coasters
Kings Island
6300 Kings Island Dr., Mason, OH
visitkingsisland.com

For roller coaster lovers, the Kings Island amusement park is the place to be. The dual-tracked Racer, with side-by-side tracks for competing trains, and Scooby Doo (today's Woodstock Express), are the park's oldest, debuting on May 27, 1972, at the park's grand opening. When the Racer was featured on a 1973 episode of TV's *The Brady Bunch*, it elevated the park into national attention and sparked broad interest in roller coasters.

The Beast nailed down Kings Island's reputation for these thrilling rides. The wooden roller coaster debuted in 1979 as the tallest, fastest, and longest in the world. It was designed by the park's lead engineers, Al Collins and Jeff Gramke, working with renowned coaster architect John C. Allen (1907–1979). A Kings Island publicist heard construction crews calling it "a beast of a project," and that became the ride's name.

It is still the longest: 7,539 feet, racing across 35 acres of hilly terrain. It has ranked consistently in the top 10 of wooden coasters worldwide. Now in its fifth decade, the area's most beloved roller coaster has thrilled more than 50 million riders with one of the longest ride times anywhere: four minutes and ten seconds.

Photo courtesy of Kings Island.

EAST

Oldest Indigenous Peoples

Serpent Mound Historical Site

3850 State Rte. 73, Peebles, OH
ohiohistory.org/visit/museum-and-site-locator/serpent-mound

Indigenous peoples likely lived in the region 12,000 years ago, but the earliest historic record of a native culture is the Adena people, who flourished from roughly 800 BC to 100 AD, the Early Woodland period. Another culture, the Hopewell, were present from 100 BC to 400 AD. More recent was the Fort Ancient culture, local residents from 1000 to 1650 AD. The Adena and the Hopewell interred their dead in burial mounds, some still evident in the 19th century in southwest Ohio. But there were no efforts at preservation, and the growing city was built over them.

Near the town of Peebles in rural Adams County, about 70 miles east of Cincinnati, is the Great Serpent Mound, one of the world's largest effigy mounds, earthen structures in the shape of animals. Built on a spur of rock overlooking Brush Creek, a 1,376-foot curling snake with a coiled tail terminates with a triangular formation, variously interpreted as a serpent's head or eye, an egg being swallowed, or perhaps the sun. Recent archeological findings (2014) suggest it was constructed around 321 BC by the Adena people.

Photo courtesy of Getty Images.

First recorded in 1848, the site was excavated in 1883 by anthropologist Frederic Ward Putnam (1839–1915), the "Father of American Archaeology" from Boston's Peabody Museum. No artifacts were found, but Putnam's attention led to the mound becoming the oldest privately funded archaeological preserve in the United States. Today, the site is maintained by the Ohio History Connection. It's open year-round for general visitation. Extended dawn-to-dusk hours are offered on the solstices and equinoxes.

Other historic indigenous tribes who lived in or near the Ohio River valley were the Miami, Shawnee, Ottawa, Wyandot, Huron, and Delaware tribes.

=1788

OLDEST NEIGHBORHOODS
COLUMBIA-TUSCULUM
Along Eastern Avenue

Cincinnati's Columbia-Tusculum neighborhood, six miles east of downtown, began as Columbia on November 18, 1788, when 26 people, including four women and two children, landed flatboats at the junction of the Little Miami and Ohio rivers. They established the first settlement in southwest Ohio. By 1790, there were 15 homes. The community also has the area's oldest cemetery, the Pioneer Memorial Cemetery (333 Wilmer Ave.). Its first burial in 1790 was rumored to be a soldier killed in a tavern brawl. The cemetery is listed on the National Register of Historic Places under its original name, Columbia Baptist Cemetery. In 1871, Columbia-Tusculum became a Cincinnati city neighborhood. Today, several blocks of its streets are admired for their charming "Painted Ladies," colorfully decorated Victorian homes.

Photo courtesy of Rick Pender.

On December 28, 1788, a party of 11 families led by Colonel Robert Patterson (1753–1827) arrived at a site on the north bank of the Ohio River across from Kentucky's Licking River, today's boundary between Covington and Newport on the south bank. The new Ohio settlement briefly was named Losantiville, a cobbled-together name supposedly meaning, "the city opposite the mouth of the Licking River." In 1789, a military structure, Fort Washington, was built. Typically, it supported a garrison of 300 soldiers, commanded by General Arthur St. Clair (1737–1818), the Northwest Territory's first governor. The fort was abandoned in 1803. In 1790, St. Clair renamed the city Cincinnati, after the Society of the Cincinnati, a patriotic organization honoring George Washington founded by officers of the Continental Army who served with him during the Revolutionary War. By 1820, Cincinnati's population was nearly 10,000.

Pioneer Memorial Cemetery. Photo courtesy of Rick Pender.

Newport, established around 1791 by General James Taylor Jr., was the earliest settlement across the Ohio River. He recognized the business potential of a location at the confluence of the Ohio and Licking rivers. The city was incorporated in 1795.

Oldest Underground Railroad Safe House

John Rankin House

6152 Rankin Hill Road, Ripley, OH
ohiohistorycentral.org/w/rankin_house

John P. Parker Museum & Historical Society

300 N Front St., Ripley
johnparkerhouse.net

On New Year's Eve 1821, John Rankin (1793–1886), an abolitionist and Presbyterian minister, rowed his family across the icy Ohio River from Kentucky to the town of Ripley, about 50 miles east of Cincinnati. By 1828, he had built a modest house on a hilltop, large enough to house Rankin, his wife, and their 13 children. He founded a Presbyterian academy for boys; in 1838, one of its students was the young Ulysses S. Grant. Rankin's writings and work in the anti-slavery movement influenced many prominent abolitionists before and during the Civil War.

Rankin's home also was a frequent "station" on the Underground Railroad for as many as 2,000 enslaved people seeking freedom, sometimes as many as 12 at a time. Atop the hill overlooking the river, the house had a lantern or a candle in a window that signaled to runaway slaves when it was safe to cross the river and guided them to temporary safety in the free state of Ohio. Today, Rankin's home is a historic house museum.

Ripley's 55-acre historic district is listed on the National Register of Historic Places. In Ripley in the 1830s, author **Harriet Beecher Stowe** (1811–1896) heard the story of Eliza, a slave who escaped across the frozen river. Eliza's experience inspired a character in *Uncle Tom's Cabin* (1852), Stowe's influential novel. The historic town also was home to a one-time slave, John P. Parker (1827–1900), an African American inventor and active "conductor" for the Underground Railroad. He helped hundreds of escaped slaves make their way to freedom.

Thanks to the writings of John Rankin, Ripley became renowned in the 19th century for its strong beliefs in the abolition of slavery. Proximity to the Ohio River made it a frequent stop for runaway slaves traveling north from Kentucky.

Photo courtesy of Getty Images.

Oldest Literary Home
Harriet Beecher Stowe House
2950 Gilbert Ave., Walnut Hills
stowehousecincy.org

Harriet Beecher (1811–1896) was 22 when she came from Connecticut to live in Cincinnati in 1832. The Reverend Lyman Beecher (1775–1863), her father, was the head of Lane Seminary, and they lived in the home provided by the religious training institution. In 1836, she married Calvin Stowe (1802–1886), a professor at Lane, where the issue of abolition was debated contentiously. She gathered personal impressions of slavery at a Kentucky slave auction, and she heard a story told at the seminary by abolitionist **John Rankin** about a slave who escaped across the frozen Ohio River. Harriet Beecher Stowe's writing career began with *Uncle Tom's Cabin* (1852), which included the story of an escaped slave, Eliza. Her book was a catalyst that inflamed the passions that sparked the Civil War. When she met President Abraham Lincoln in 1862, he reportedly teased her, saying, "So you are the little woman who wrote the book that started this great war." Her novel has been published in more than 75 languages.

The Beecher family frequently housed fugitive slaves at the house on Gilbert Avenue. Now a history and culture museum, the house features historic exhibits about the author and her father's family. It also serves as a public meeting place, presents art exhibits, and offers classes on African American history.

Photo courtesy of Rick Pender.

OLDEST AMUSEMENT PARK
CONEY ISLAND AMUSEMENT PARK

6201 Kellogg Ave., Anderson Twp.
coneyislandpark.com

P arker's Grove, 10 miles east of downtown Cincinnati in Anderson Township, started in 1867 as an apple orchard that evolved into a picnic ground. In 1886, the park was purchased and renamed Ohio Grove, billed as "the Coney Island of the West." In 1887, the name was shortened simply to Coney Island. For many years, the Island Queen, a riverboat with five decks that could accommodate 4,000 passengers, ferried entertainment seekers from the city to Coney Island's amusement park, which included rides, attractions, and Moonlite Pavilion, a popular dance hall. Taft Broadcasting

Historic postcard.

purchased the park in 1969. In response to frequent flooding by the Ohio River, Taft decided to establish **Kings Island** (1972) north of the city, now the region's major amusement park.

However, "Old Coney" survived as a destination for picnics and family entertainment, with carnival rides and a small water park. In 2019, the park's operations were narrowed exclusively to water park amenities. The major attraction is the world's largest recirculating swimming pool, Sunlite Pool (1925), 200 feet wide and 401 feet long, with more than 300 million gallons of water. It covers two acres, more than a football field. It's certainly one of the oldest pools in Cincinnati.

Coney Island is adjacent to the **Cincinnati Symphony Orchestra's** summer home, Riverbend Music Center (opened in 1984), and Belterra Park (opened in 1925 as River Downs), where horse racing and casino gambling are the attractions.

Riverbend Music Center has two stages. The Corbett Pavilion can accommodate 20,500 concertgoers, 6,000 in reserved seats and 14,500 on the sloped lawn. The PNC Pavilion (opened in 2008) has 4,100 seats.

Oldest Candy Maker
Doscher's Candy Factory
6926 Main St., Newtown
doscherscandies.com

Peter Minges & Son Confectionery
138 W Court St.

German immigrants had a sweet tooth, making an eager audience for candy. Doscher's Candy Company was founded in 1871 by Claus Doscher (1852–1889), a young German immigrant, who came to the United States when he was just 19. He learned about candy-making from his uncles. The company was the first manufacturer of candy canes in the United States. It's also the oldest continuously operating candy company in America. Claus died at 37, but his brother, John, took over and expanded the business to include cream candies, chewing gum, maple candies, and Bon Ton chocolates. It was a multigenerational company until 2003, but its high standards have been maintained by new owners, Greg and Ronna Clark.

Candy canes made by hand with real peppermint oil in small batches always have been a principal product, but Doscher's also is known for French Chew, a chewy, nougat-like candy in various flavors. It's still made and sold in bars and bite-size minis. Once a downtown destination, Doscher's Candy Company now is located in Newtown, in an 1835 farmhouse; there's an attractive tearoom, and factory tours are available in the converted barn.

Photo courtesy of Cindy Doscher.

You can find Doscher's products and countless others at Peter Minges & Son Confectionery in downtown. Peter Minges (1887–1967) began to sell candy in 1905, at age 18. His Court Street shop is Cincinnati's oldest candy store. It feels like a step back in history, with shelves and counters stuffed with classic candies that can be purchased in bulk or by weight.

For those who can't get enough candy from Doscher's and Minges, there's more to be found at Graeter's and Aglamesis Brothers' ice cream parlors.

Peter Minges & Son Confectionery. Photo courtesy of Rick Pender.

Oldest Airport

Cincinnati Municipal Airport–Lunken Airfield

262 Wilmer Ave.
cincinnati-oh.gov/dote/
lunken-airport

Cincinnati/Northern Kentucky International Airport (CVG)

2939 Terminal Dr., Hebron, KY
CVGairport.com

Summit Park

4335 Glendale-Milford Rd., Blue Ash, OH
summitparkblueash.com

Cincinnati's airport, formally the Cincinnati/Northern Kentucky International Airport (aka CVG) is in Hebron, Kentucky, 19 miles south of downtown. It began operations in 1946. But it is not the area's oldest: that honor goes to Lunken Airfield, Cincinnati's municipal airport, five miles east of downtown, in the Little Miami River valley, near the area's **first settlement** (1788). Edmund H. Lunken (1861–1944), owner of the Lunkenheimer Co., manufacturer of steam valves, purchased 204 acres there in 1928. He donated the tract to the city for an airport.

Early aviation activities already had happened nearby in 1921, just north of Lunken's location. Charles Lindbergh landed there in 1927. The airport was dedicated in September 1930, served by Mason and Dixon Airlines, Embry-Riddle Airlines, and Universal Aviation Corporation, which soon became American Airlines. Lunken was an imperfect location: during the Ohio River's 1937 flood, it was nicknamed "sunken Lunken." Nevertheless, even after it was supplanted by CVG, Lunken continued to serve fliers: the Beatles landed there for their 1964 concert at Cincinnati Gardens, and many US presidents touched down on its runways. Today, it's served by Ultimate Air Shuttle, a regional commuter air service, and is home to many private and corporate aircraft.

The Cincinnati-Blue Ash Airport never entirely took off. Owned by Cincinnati but located in Blue Ash, Ohio, 15 miles northeast of downtown, the airfield was established in 1921 and long was envisioned as the city's primary commercial airport. But that didn't happen. Some of its property became industrial land and a golf course; Cincinnati eventually sold the balance to Blue Ash in 2012 for a mixed-use development, Summit Park, with a 153-foot tower as a tourist attraction.

Lunken Playfield, adjacent to the airport, has hiking trails that are good for walking, running, and biking. Also available are tennis courts and the Reeves public golf course, an 18-hole course and another that's 9 holes, par-3 throughout.

Photo courtesy of Rick Pender.

Oldest Drive-In Movie Theaters

Starlite Drive-In

2255 State Rte. OH-125, Amelia
starlitedriveinohio.com

Holiday Auto Theatre

1816 Old Oxford Rd., Hamilton
holidayautotheatre.com

The first US drive-in movie theater opened in 1933 in New Jersey. Greater Cincinnati's first outdoor venue for drivers to pull in, park, and watch a movie was Amelia's Starlite Drive-In, opened in 1947 by Jerry Jackson, who operated it until 1968. In the 21st century, it's still showing movies, usually double features, plus occasional live or simulcast concerts. New owners even have enabled it to serve as a temporary federal courthouse for a naturalization ceremony.

In 1948, the Hamilton Outdoor Theatre opened, north of Cincinnati. In 1951, its name was changed to the Holiday Auto Theatre. Drive-in movies boomed in the 1950s and 1960s, when there were more than 4,000 such theaters nationwide. By 2020, that number dwindled to about 350, but the Starlite Drive-In and the Holiday Auto Theatre were still at it.

Photo courtesy of starlitemovies.com.

WEST

Oldest Building
The Betts House

416 Clark St.
thebettshouse.org

Kemper Log House

Heritage Village at Sharon Woods Park
11450 Lebanon Rd., Sharonville, OH
heritagevillagecincinnati.org

The oldest building in the Cincinnati basin is at 416 Clark St. in the historic Betts-Longworth neighborhood, just east of downtown. The Betts House is, in fact, one of the oldest brick buildings in Ohio. In the early 1800s, William and Phebe Betts set aside part of their 111-acre farm for a brickyard that provided building materials for Cincinnati's early settlers. The couple was on the leading edge of a trend to build more permanent structures than the log-and-frame homes of the era on adjacent land first owned by developer **Nicholas Longworth**. This is the city's earliest surviving brick building, built in 1804. The Betts family inhabited it for four generations.

Surrounded by Victorian homes from later in the 19th century, the Betts House inspired the establishment of the Betts-Longworth Historic District in 1983. Since 1994, the house has been owned by the National Society of Colonial Dames of America, also serving as the society's headquarters. It is open to the public as a house museum, with exhibits and programs focused on historic buildings and Cincinnati's history from the early 19th century.

The Betts House (1804). Photo courtesy of Rick Pender.

Another early house now resides in the Heritage Village in Sharon Woods Park. Pastor James Kemper's log house (1804) was built in Walnut Hills for his family of 15 children and for a long time was on display at the Cincinnati Zoo. Kemper rode a horse through the wilderness to deliver sermons. His church, a simple, rustic frame building, was on Fourth Street near Main Street, with pews made from planks. Congregants were expected to bring rifles to fend off attacks by the indigenous Shawnee people; if they failed to do so, they were fined.

Nicholas Longworth became an early Cincinnati millionaire through land speculation. In addition to land in the Betts-Longworth District, he had property in Mount Adams where Cincinnati's original observatory was situated in 1843.

OLDEST MUSEUM
CINCINNATI MUSEUM OF NATURAL HISTORY & SCIENCE

Cincinnati Museum Center
1301 Western Ave.
cincymuseum.org

The Cincinnati Museum of Natural History & Science has a history going back more than two centuries, making it Cincinnati's oldest museum. It began as the Western Museum (1818), founded by physician and scientist **Dr. Daniel Drake**. He hired John James Audubon (1785–1851), a Frenchman who immigrated to the United States in 1803, as its first paid employee. Drake encouraged Audubon to compile his legendary, color-plate book of illustrations, *The Birds of America*, published in sections from 1827 to 1838.

Photo courtesy of Cincinnati Museum Center.

Drake went on to establish the Western Academy of Natural Sciences in 1835, incorporating collections from the Western Museum. This organization evolved into the Cincinnati Society of Natural History in the 1860s. In 1958, the Natural History Museum moved to its own building on Gilbert Avenue, adjacent to Eden Park. Today, the new studios of WCPO-TV stand on this spot. Mastodon statues that once grazed along Gilbert Avenue can be found today at the Museum Center's Geier Collections and Research Center (760 W Fifth St.). The museum was known for its educational outreach, as well as for a planetarium and a realistically recreated cavern. In 1990, it became a tenant in the one-time **Union Terminal** when that historic structure became the **Cincinnati Museum Center.** In its new home, the cavern became "The Cave," 500 feet of twists and turns, inspired by Kentucky's Mammoth Cave.

Attendance and membership grew rapidly at the Museum Center. Today, it attracts more than 1.5 million guests annually. Fans of dinosaurs especially are attracted to new skeleton and fossil installations made possible by an extensive renovation and expansion in 2018: the Dinosaur Hall features skeletons of the *Galeamopus* and *Daspletosaurus*, as well as the singular *Tovosaurus*, the only one of its kind on display.

Dr. Daniel Drake's interests were not limited to medicine. Considered the "Benjamin Franklin of the West," he advocated social reforms, contributed to geology, botany, and meteorology. He also proposed the buckeye tree as Ohio's state emblem.

OLDEST TRAIN STATION
CINCINNATI MUSEUM CENTER

1301 Western Ave.
cincymuseum.org

Cincinnati Union Terminal, built in 1933, replaced five downtown stations that had served seven railroads. A fine example of Art Deco architecture, it was designed by Alfred T. Fellheimer (1875–1959), who also designed New York City's Grand Central Station. The terminal's distinctive architecture, interior design, and history made it a National Historic Landmark (1977). Its breathtaking, half-dome rotunda features mosaic murals by Winold Reiss (1886–1953) depicting Cincinnati history.

The north front façade features a relief by Maxfield Keck (1880–1943) of the mythological god Hermes, the Roman deity of commerce and communications and messenger of the gods. Low on the wall is inscribed the year 1931, when the building's cornerstone was laid. On the south façade a female figure, Transportation, bears a winged globe on her back and a locomotive at her feet.

Union Terminal was busy in the 1940s as soldiers went off to war and returned from World War II. But train services were on the decline; the terminal closed in

*Photo courtesy of
Cincinnati Museum Center.*

Photo courtesy of Cincinnati Museum Center.

1972. In 1980, a developer converted it into an unsuccessful shopping mall.

In 1985, the Museum of Natural History & Science and the Cincinnati Historical Society merged and planned to relocate to the terminal. The Cincinnati Museum Center opened in 1990. It contained a local history museum with an exhibit of the 19th-century riverfront, a historical library, a natural history museum with a reproduction of a limestone cavern, and an Omnimax® Theater. (Amtrak restored passenger service in 1991.) The Children's Museum opened in 1998; the Nancy & David Wolf Holocaust & Humanity Center was added in 2019. A $228 million physical renovation of the building, funded by county sales tax proceeds, was conducted from 2016 to 2018. The Museum Center has become one of the city's greatest tourist attractions.

Before various rail lines serving Cincinnati were consolidated at the Union Terminal, travelers often had to drag themselves and their baggage from one far-flung station to another to make connections.

OLDEST PIZZA PARLOR
LAROSA'S

2411 Boudinot Ave., Westwood
larosas.com, larosasmvp.com

In the early 1950s, Buddy LaRosa made pizzas for the annual summer festival at San Antonio Italian Catholic Church with his Aunt Dena's recipe. They were a hit, leading LaRosa to open his first pizzeria, called Papa Gino's, in 1954 with three friends. LaRosa's Sicilian-born father told his son he was crazy: many Americans had not heard of pizza. But the young entrepreneur bought out his partners before long and changed the name to LaRosa's Pizzeria. Today, his sons run the business; between the family and franchise owners, now more than 60 pizzerias serve neighborhoods in Cincinnati, Northern Kentucky, Southeast Indiana, Dayton, and Columbus. Its popularity in Greater Cincinnati exceeds that of several national chains.

LaRosa's signature pizza is made with the thick, sweet sauce that Aunt Dena originated. The menu also includes appetizers, hoagies—including one called The Baked Buddy—as well as calzones, salads, and pastas.

The pizzeria's popularity has been extended by its involvement in neighborhoods. LaRosa responded gratefully to coaches and players from several high schools who came forward to help with cleanup after an April 1973 fire that nearly ruined his original pizzeria. He created a weekly recognition program for outstanding high school athletes, and memorialized some of them with his Buddy LaRosa High School Sports Hall of Fame. Boudinot Avenue remains LaRosa's flagship location.

Photo courtesy of Rick Pender.

OLDEST EDUCATIONAL TV STATION

WCET-TV

1223 Central Pkwy.
CETconnect.org

Cincinnati's oldest non-commercial television station, WCET, has a more expansive credit: It was granted the first non-commercial educational broadcast license by the Federal Communications Commission on March 11, 1955. It actually began to broadcast on July 26, 1954, from Dexter Hall, a converted space on the third floor of **Cincinnati Music Hall**, what today is called Corbett Tower. On UHF channel 48, it was viewable only to a few hundred people who could receive programming on that frequency. The first program was *Tel-A-Story*, a 30-minute reading program produced by the Cincinnati Public Library.

Programs aired from Music Hall until 1959, when WCET moved to

Photo courtesy of WCET.

WLWT-TV's former studios on Chickasaw Street near the University of Cincinnati. In 1976, the station moved to its own facility, the Crosley Telecommunications Center, on Central Parkway across from the west façade of Cincinnati Music Hall. In 2009, WCET's owner, the Greater Cincinnati Television Educational Foundation, formed an umbrella nonprofit organization, Public Media Connect, with Greater Dayton Public Television.

WCET provided the first local, on-demand, classroom program for schools via cable TV in 1983, the first instructional resource guides for teachers in 1985, and the first 24/7 local arts channel, CET Arts in 2010. The station produced Lilias Folan's *Lilias, Yoga & You* for PBS stations nationwide from 1974 until 1999. For more than 50 years, the annual "Action Auction" has been the station's largest and most successful fundraising event.

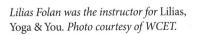

Lilias Folan was the instructor for Lilias, Yoga & You. *Photo courtesy of WCET.*

SOURCES

Wendy Hart Beckman, *Founders and Famous Families: Cincinnati* (Covington, Kentucky: Clerisy Press, 2014).

Joyce V. B. Cauffield and Carolyn E. Banfield, co-editors, *The River Book: Cincinnati and the Ohio* (Cincinnati: The Program for Cincinnati, 1981).

Mary Anna DuSablon, *Walking the Steps of Cincinnati* (Athens: Ohio University Press, 1998, 2014).

Luke Feck, *Yesterday's Cincinnati* (Special Bicentennial Edition) (Cincinnati: Writer's Digest Books, 1975, 1987).

Cincinnati Historical Society, *Queen City Tour: A Self-Guided Driving Tour* (Cincinnati: Cincinnati Museum Center for Natural and Cultural History and Science, 1996).

Geoffrey J. Giglierano and Deborah A. Overmyer, with Fredric L. Propas, *The Bicentennial Guide To Greater Cincinnati: A Portrait of Two Hundred Years* (Cincinnati: The Cincinnati Historical Society, 1988).

Kevin Grace and Tom White, *Cincinnati Cemeteries: The Queen City Underground* (Charleston, S.C.: Arcadia Publishing, 2004).

Daniel Hurley and Paul A. Tenkotte, *Cincinnati: The Queen City, 225th Anniversary Edition*, Fourth Edition, (Cincinnati: Cincinnati Museum Center, 2014).

Blanche M. G. Linden, *Spring Grove: Celebrating 150 Years* (Cincinnati: Spring Grove Cemetery & Arboretum and the Cincinnati Historical Society, 1995).

Michael D. Morgan, *Cincinnati Beer* (Charleston, South Carolina: American Palate/History Press, 2019).

Michael D. Morgan, *Over-the-Rhine: When Beer Was King* (Charleston, South Carolina: History Press, 2010).

Bill Oeters and Nancy Gulick, *Miami and Erie Canal* (Charleston, South Carolina: Arcadia Publishing, 2014).

William F. Poole, *The Tyler Davidson Fountain Given by Mr. Henry Probasco to the City of Cincinnati* (Cincinnati: Robert Clarke & Co., 1891; reprinted by the Cincinnati Historical Society, 1988).

Gregory Parker Rogers, *Fountain Square and the Genius of Water: The Heart of Cincinnati* (Charleston, South Carolina: History Press, 2013).

Steven J. Rolfes, *Cincinnati Landmarks* (Charleston, South Carolina: Arcadia Press, 2012).

Iola Silberstein, *Cincinnati Then and Now* (Cincinnati: The League of Women Voters of Cincinnati Area, 1982).

Sarah Stephens, *Cincinnati's Brewing History* (Charleston, South Carolina: Arcadia Press, 2010).

Jeff Suess, *Cincinnati: An Illustrated Timeline* (St. Louis: Reedy Press, 2020).

Jeff Suess, *Cincinnati: Then and Now* (London: Pavilion Books, 2018).

Jeff Suess, *Hidden History of Cincinnati* (Charleston, S.C.: The History Press, 2016).

Don Heinrich Tolzmann, *Cincinnati's Beer Barons in the Golden Age of Brewing* (Milford, Ohio: Little Miami Publishing, 2019).

Don Heinrich Tolzmann, *Christian Moerlein: The Man and His Brewery* (Milford, Ohio: Little Miami Publishing, 2012).

Don Heinrich Tolzmann, *German Cincinnati* (Charleston. S.C.: Arcadia Publishing, 2005).

Daniel Hurley and Paul A. Tenkotte, *Cincinnati: The Queen City, 225th Anniversary Edition*, Fourth Edition, (Cincinnati: Cincinnati Museum Center, 2014). Entirely visible online, index is 172-179. https://www.yumpu.com/en/document/read/62138778/cincinnati-the-queen-city-22th-anniversary-edition.

INDEX